The Iban of Sarawak
Chronicle of a vanishing world

VINSON H. SUTLIVE, JR.
The College of William and Mary in Virginia

WAVELAND
PRESS, INC.
Prospect Heights, Illinois

For information about this book, write or call:

Waveland Press, Inc.
P.O. Box 400
Prospect Heights, Illinois 60070
(708) 634-0081

To Joanne, Vins, Susan, and Tom.

Cover: An Iban man weaves a fishnet (*nyambong jala*). The expression *nyambong jala* is used to describe the tracing of genealogies by Iban upon meeting, and as an analogy for the cultural construction of the Iban world. (Courtesy of Louis R. Dennis)

Copyright © 1978 by Vinson H. Sutlive, Jr.
1988 reissued with changes by Waveland Press, Inc.

ISBN 0-88133-357-3

Printed in the United States of America

7 6 5 4 3 2

The Iban of Sarawak

Foreword

Iban culture was forged in the sacred hills of inland Borneo. It was constructed on the principle of mobility: a mobility both in fact and in spirit. The shifting cultivation of dry rice, requiring long periods of fallow, made it necessary to seek new lands, and first among the qualities requisite for a person of stature was the capacity to pioneer new lands. Iban expansion was accomplished at the expense of neighboring peoples so that also among the necessary virtues was the courage to engage in head hunting.

Wherever geographic mobility is found, there also one tends to find social mobility—and this is the case among the Iban. With such mobility, in turn, is associated a pattern of personal independence and individualism—qualities that even Iban children display.

Individualism and personal mobility must be held in check, for the Iban, like people everywhere, are mutually dependent. It is a seeming paradox that a society built upon mobility should engage in one of the most elaborate of domestic architectures to be found in tribal society: the long house. These structures may extend over 250 yards and include up to 70 households, knitting together a community physically as well as socially. Thus mutuality in economic activities as well as in military ventures is assured.

Sutlive shows us not only these structured elements, but demonstrates how an elaborate set of beliefs and rituals binds together the individualistic Iban into a strong community. He shows us also how this culture fares under the impact of westernization—how the individualism and opportunism makes for adaptation to the new circumstances, but also how these new circumstances destroy the very source of these qualities.

The Iban of Sarawak addresses itself to the ecology of cultures not in the narrow sense of production and the requisite patterns of institutionalized collaboration, but in the broader sense of recognizing that these activities involve the structuring of sentiments and the inculcation of personality attributes. We see in the rich metaphors of Iban culture and psychological dimension of the ecological forces to which the Iban are subject.

Walter Goldschmidt

Acknowledgements

I am indebted beyond expression to friends and critics who through their insights and suggestions have made this book possible.

The people of Rumah Nyala, Imba, Nyelang, and Gaong provided me with unstinting hospitality. Together with Iban of other houses they patiently answered my questions and even managed to "ignore" me occasionally so that I could watch the more normal flow of life as a nonobtrusive observer—if a six-foot, 180-pound American can ever be such!

I am grateful to colleagues in the Methodist Church of Sarawak for their friendship; to the Board of Global Ministries of the United Methodist Church for support; to the National Science Foundation for a dissertation grant; to Anyau Bakit, Benedict Sandin, Lucas Chin, Tuba', Ampan, Ganai, and Enchul for long talks and other resources; to Shearon Vaughn for the maps, drawings, and charts; to Lyle Rosbotham and Jim Williams for aid with the photographs; and to Susan Glendinning for typing the manuscript.

Finally, I want to acknowledge the advice of my instructors at the University of Pittsburgh, especially Alexander Spoehr, Leonard Plotnicov, and Keith Brown, and the encouragement of colleagues in the Department of Anthropology, The College of William and Mary.

Preface 1988

The dramatic and wide-ranging changes occurring among the Iban are representative of similar developments in the lives of tribal people throughout the world. The old is going, in many instances, gone. Traditional patterns of social organization as well as familiar beliefs and behaviors will soon be no more.

The Iban of Sarawak, with an Epilogue based upon research conducted in 1984 and 1987, describes the continuing movements of Iban into Sarawak's cities, and their new strategies of adaptation.

Contents

INTRODUCTION

"The Universe has as many different centers as there are living beings in it. Each of us is a center of the Universe. . . ." (Aleksandr I. Solzhenitsyn, *The Gulag Archipelago*)

The purpose of this study is to analyze the world of the Iban as it has developed in the hills of Borneo, and the changes it has undergone as the Iban have moved into new settings.

The Iban have placed themselves squarely at the center of their universe, thus sharing a widespread human propensity for ethnocentrism. Each longhouse community has been a microcosm of the Iban world on which the sun, moon, and stars have been focused. The cosmology of the Iban has been Ptolemaic as other societies have orbited them and then been drawn within the sphere of Iban ideas and activities.

Predictably, Iban means "human" and the name-bearers are "proud of it" (McKinley, 1973). Equally to be expected, the Iban have considered members of other ethnic groups as less than human because of their differences. Such groups have existed to be brought within the domain of humanity, i.e., Ibanness, through the universe-extending activities of raiding and head-hunting. Myth and ritual have legitimized the world view of the Iban whose unassailable confidence has made them venturesome and optimistic, the most aggressive of the peoples native to Borneo. Numbering 300,000 of Sarawak's one million people, the Iban are the largest of the state's indigenous groups.

Iban also may mean "wanderer." For centuries they have moved through the hills of Borneo, farming dry rice, gathering, hunting, and fishing, expanding in territory as well as numbers. During the past century they have moved into the delta plains of the Rejang and other river valleys, where they now grow wet rice, rubber, and pepper, and work for wages. Within the past two decades several thousand Iban have moved into the towns of Sarawak—Kuching and Kapit, Simanggang and Sibu—and a few have moved on to Singapore, West Malaysia, Australia, the United Kingdom, and the United States.

The expanding world of the Iban has reflected and reinforced the norms of social and cultural mobility. Pioneers became folk heroes who helped ensure the survival of their people by breaching the boundaries of the known world and opening up new land. The small nuclear family was selected as the fundamental unit of Iban society. And the longhouse—difficult to describe and impossible to imagine—was an eco-ritual center of existence to be occupied for several years before being abandoned as families moved into new areas.

The travels and territorial expansion of the Iban have brought them into contact with other ethnic groups: Malays, Chinese, Bukitan, Melanau, Kayan, Europeans, and others. Confronted with beliefs and behavior different from their own, the Iban have eschewed insularity as they have attempted to come to terms with the plurality of life-worlds. That they have been remarkably successful is apparent in the persistence of many features of traditional Iban culture, including the fierce pride shown in their own identity.

Iban culture expresses the philosophy that the attitudes of men are ambivalent and that life is ambiguous. Thus, the Iban have peopled their world with gods who are to be followed because they are helpful, and with evil spirits who are to be feared because they are harmful. This philosophical orientation has helped immunize the Iban to traditional tensions, such as the conflict between the rituals of individuation and the demands of subservience to the group, and to stresses in situations of change, such as the abandonment of "the ways of the ancestors" for the acceptance of institutions of other societies.

The Iban are one of the best-described societies of hill farmers in the world. Derek Freeman's outstanding studies (listed in the bibliography) have put the students of man in his debt. But the Iban no longer perceive themselves exclusively or even predominantly as hill farmers; they now are people of all work, and include doctors, lawyers, and Members of Parliament.

The Iban have shown what has been described by some social scientists as an amazing ability to adjust to new environments. This ability may be dismissed as nothing more than adaptability common to all human beings; to do so, however, overlooks the fact that, unlike some societies whose members have been overwhelmed in situations of change, the Iban have suffered neither a debilitating social disorganization nor a traumatic cultural disorientation. Rather, with a remarkably "liberal conservatism" they have shown a positive inclination toward change which has predisposed them to seek new experiences and to think new thoughts, quite purposefully engaging in "the dialectics of social life" (Murphy, 1971).

This book is based upon research conducted among the Iban of the Sibu District between 1969 and 1972. The Sibu District is an irregularly shaped political unit (see map) of 1,305 square miles. The district is divided into urban (20 square miles) and rural (1,285 square miles) areas. The town of Sibu, with a population of 70,000, is the political, economic, welfare, and entertainment center of the vast Rejang Valley with a population of more than 220,000 people.

My fieldwork concentrated on Iban in rural and urban settings. In the former setting my studies were on the communities of Rumah ("house" [of]) Nyala, Rumah Imba, Rumah Nyelang, and Rumah Gaong, each community being named for the "headman of the house" *(tuai rumah)*. Rumah Gaong is the least acculturated of the four communities, and together with data collected from more remote upriver communities, provided information that I have used in the description of the more traditional hill culture. Until eight years ago Rumah Gaong was relatively isolated from external influences, when compared to other Iban communities in the district. Located at the headwaters of the Sengan River, Rumah Gaong was accessible only by river travel or footpath, requiring half a day's travel time or longer to reach Sibu. It is important to note that even though Rumah Gaong is within the Sibu District, in many respects—construction and appearance of house, dress, behavior, and rituals—the community retains certain features of aboriginal culture which have been lost by presumably more "traditional" upriver communities whose members have greater and more frequent exposure to external influences.

The reader should understand that the Iban hill culture is an analytical construct based upon observations of Rumah Gaong and other less acculturated longhouses. I traveled and lived among the Iban for eleven years between 1957 and 1972, and the account of the hill culture is a distillation of innumerable impressions as well as my field notes.

Rumah Imba and Rumah Nyelang lie about halfway between Rumah Gaong and Sibu, off a spur of the Sibu-Kuching Road. These communities combine folk traditions and elements of modern society. Some units in both houses were built by the residents, others by professional Malay carpenters. The people in both communities farm dry and wet rice. About half of the families in both communities are Christian, and all make use of shamanic or Christian rituals in the treatment of illness.

Rumah Nyala can be reached by a five-minute walk from the jetty or end of a road, each about half an hour's travel time from Sibu. Although the residents of Rumah Nyala retain longhouse domicile, the community is one of the most acculturated, decidedly different from Rumah Gaong and upriver Iban. Long and frequent exposure to the people of Sibu has made them more sophisticated in their dealings with members of other societies, leading more conservative Iban to ask whether the people of Rumah Nyala are still "real" Iban? No such question exists in the mind of the residents of Rumah Nyala, despite the fact that some of their members have moved into Sibu and others commute to their work in town each day.

While there are many similarities between the Iban who are the subjects of this study and those of the Sut River described by Freeman, there also are important differences, reflecting in part the earlier time when Freeman's study was made and in part the different settings. Unlike the far more isolated Iban of the Sut—who today are much like Freeman found them twenty-five years ago and, in their extreme conservatism, are atypical of the majority of Iban who are open to change—the

Iban of the Sibu District have accommodated to numerous foreign influences, especially within the past twenty years.

Today few Iban in the district live more than two hours from Sibu, which is accessible by private boat, car, bicycle, public launch, ferry, and taxi. Radios are found in every longhouse and provide daily communication from the state and abroad. Contacts with residents of Sibu and tourists have whetted the appetites of Iban for knowledge of peoples whose ways are different from their own. I have spent many nights attempting to describe television, as yet not introduced into Sarawak, and to answer questions about moonshots.

In addition to the intensive study of the four communities already named, I conducted censuses of thirty-three other longhouses in the Sibu District. The use of censuses made by district administrators in 1958 and 1966 provided information for the study of changes in longhouse organization and family structure.

In the town of Sibu I administered questionnaires to a random sample of 200 Iban in order to determine the areas from which they were coming, motives for moving to town, employment, and persistence of kin-ties and cultural norms. I collected life histories of nine Iban in order to gain further insight into the circumstances of the urban migrants.

Although the term "Iban" is used generally in this study to describe members of a society who share a common language (with several dialects), common principles of social organization, and common norms, and while much that is contained herein is applicable to Iban in other parts of Sarawak, this is a study of the Iban of the Sibu District. I am aware that anecdotal vetoes may be adduced to numerous points, for the Iban show great diversity. I can readily accept as correct objections that "the Iban of such-and-such a place are not like that," and acknowledge the particularistic character of my study. A perceptive Iban once said, "All of us Iban, in every house, are different." *(Samoa kami Iban, alam tiap buah rumah, sigi' lain.)*

The spelling of Iban words follows the orthography devised by the Inter-Church Committee on Translation. The reader may find it helpful to remember that the following letters are pronounced as in the examples: /a/ as in "father;" /e/ as in "happen," i.e., as a schwa; /u/ in first syllables as in "rumor," in other syllables as in "put." Generally, ultimate and penultimate syllables are stressed and nasals such as /n/ or /ng/ mark the beginning of syllables rather than their ending as in English. Glottalization, the cutting off of wind by the glottis as in the English negative "uh-uh," occurs commonly in Iban after vowels in final position and is indicated by the apostrophe (/'/) as in *sigi'* above.

All monetary figures are in United States currency (reflecting the author's ethnocentrism) based on an exchange rate of 2.75 Malaysian dollars to one United States dollar.

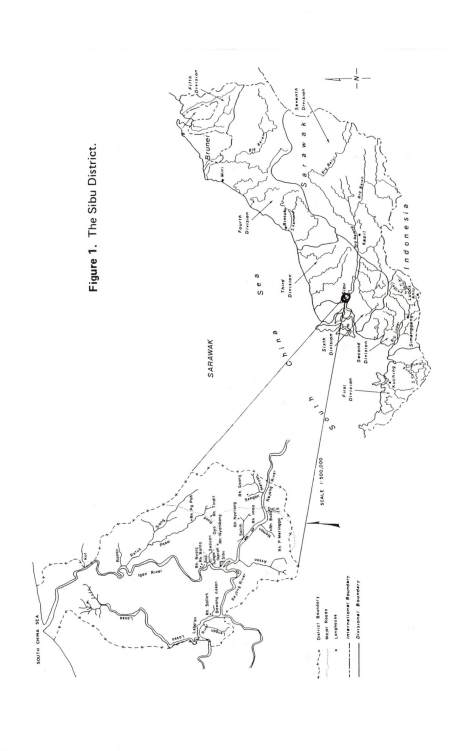

Figure 1. The Sibu District.

Figure 1. The Sibu District.

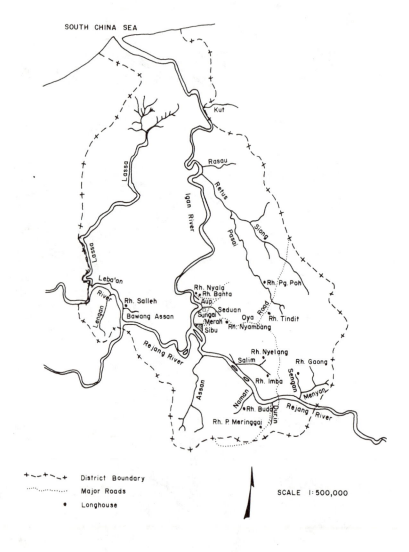

SOUTH CHINA SEA

Kut

Rasau

Lassa

Igan River

Retus

Pasai

Siong

Leba'an

Rh. Nyala
Rh. Banta
Aup.

•Rh. Pg. Poh

Lengan River

Rh. Salleh

Seduan

Bawang Assan

Sungai
Merah •
Sibu

Oya
Rh. Nyambang

Oya Road

Rh. Tindit

Lassa

Rejang River

Rh. Nyelang
Salim

Rh. Gaong

Rh. Imba

Sengan

Menyan

Assan

Naman

Durin

Rejang River

•Rh. Budu

Rh. P. Meringgai

+—+—+ District Boundary
.... Major Roads
• Longhouse

SCALE 1:500,000

8

Chapter 1

THE SETTING

Natural conditions of Borneo have had marked influences on the Iban. As they have adapted to a habitat with distinct zones, the Iban have developed a variety of responses, technical, ritual, and ideational. These responses have been implemented in the techniques and rituals designed to acquire the food and other materials considered necessary for life. The responses have been evident in the different ways in which the Iban have learned to cope with the various environmental influences to which they have been subjected. They have been expressed in the remarkable sensitization of the Iban to virtually every part of this environment, and in turn, encoded in a vast oral literature.

The Iban have built their world out of the natural, social, and metasocial orders to which they have perceived themselves as belonging. Plants, animals, hills, sun, moon, stars, ancestral spirits, and other groups have been brought together in the ethnoscience and mythology by which the Iban have developed and manipulated the symbols which have helped them understand their world and rationalize their behavior.

In order to understand the distinctive ways of life of the Iban it is necessary for us to consider some of the characteristics of the settings in which they have lived. This is not to imply that the Iban culture can be understood simply in terms of environment, but most certainly it cannot be understood apart from it. In fact, as we shall see, it has been the interplay between the Iban and their environment, the attitudes that they developed about certain areas, and their determination to control those areas at almost any price which have set the Iban off from other Bornean groups.

TOPOGRAPHY

Topographically, Sarawak includes three units. The boundary to the south is a mountainous range which forms the watershed and is part of the central mountain range of Borneo. These mountains vary from 4,000 to 6,000 feet in Sarawak, climaxing in the northeast in Mount Kinabalu, the highest point in the adjoining state of Sabah and Southeast Asia at 13,451 feet.

Below the mountains lies a broad belt of hill country. Most of the hills are less than 1,000 feet high, and until recently have been the typical occupation zone of the Iban. The hills are cut by numerous valleys formed by swift-flowing waters that run off the mountain range. In upland areas these valleys are narrow and their flanks steep. As a result, the amount of flatland available for cultivation is severely limited, with many of the hills so steep that even terracing has been judged impractical if not impossible.

The third unit is a broad plain that has been built up by vast amounts of sediment—soils and plant materials—swept down-river by the hundreds of streams and rivers flowing down the hillsides. This plain continues to extend seaward between five and thirty feet per year. The plain rises only a few feet above sea level and varies considerably in width, reaching a width of fifty miles or more in the lower valleys of the Baram, Rejang, Saribas, and Lupar rivers.

DRAINAGE AND EROSION

Sarawak is marked by numerous streams and rivers, many of which are navigable and continue to provide the chief means of travel. The major ones flow from the northern slopes of the mountain range westward or northwestward to the South China Sea. In the upland valleys, rivers rush through steep gorges and over awesome rapids, at times making travel hazardous if not impossible. If the water is too low, travel is difficult since the boats must be pulled over the shallows. On my last trip, in July 1972, the water in the Menuan, a tributary of the Rejang below Kapit, was so low that my two Iban traveling companions and I spent more time dragging the boat than we did riding in it. On the other hand, if the waters are too high, huge boulders which create the rapids are submerged, but just how deeply is an uncertainty. Thus, only the most skilled boatmen—and sometimes not even they—will attempt to negotiate the Pelagus Rapids of the Rejang above Kapit, where white water breaks over house-sized boulders. In high waters, treacherous whirlpools up to 50 feet across form, and the unwary boatman may find himself quickly caught in their pull.

In the broad delta plains the rivers meander sluggishly, dividing into numerous distributaries. Drainage is poor and the water table frequently lies only a few inches below the ground. As a result, much of the plain is characterized by swamps and underground streams which have played havoc with recent road-building schemes. For example, when the Oya Road leading from Sibu was under construction, a large section was washed away. When an Iban and I topped the crest of a hill and saw the rushing water that had broken through the road, we felt as if we had come upon an inland sea. Needless to say, crossing the river with our packs and bicycles over the temporary log bridge was an exciting experience.

On account of the extreme flatness of the plains, inland areas as far as 170 miles from the coast are affected by the tides. Evidence of tides is most apparent during the dry season when the level of the Rejang at Kapit may rise as much as two feet. On the Jih River below Kanowit, I quite literally have boated through the treetops when high tides met the rain-swollen river, and on other occasions have helped pull our boat over the stumps and logs which litter the channel's bottom when the river was drained by a receding tide. The force of tides in the constricting banks of the Lupar Valley sometimes forms bores or tidal floods, walls of water rising several feet in height.

Erosion is particularly prominent in the hilly areas where soils have been exposed by farmers. Removal of the vegetation has led to the runoff of soluble nutrients through erosion and the downward movement of such nutrients through leaching, about which we shall say more later.

CLIMATE

Lying just north of the equator, Sarawak shares many features with other areas of the humid tropics. For example, temperatures are uniformly high the year around, and daily differences are greater than seasonal variations. The annual rainfall is variable, but always heavy and in excess of 100 inches. Visitors from temperate countries comment on the mugginess because of the humidity, which is generally high. During the short dry season, however, the heat becomes so oppressive that visitors—and some residents—begin wishing for rain.

The average length of day varies little throughout the year because of Sarawak's proximity to the equator. With a regularity which surprises newcomers, the sun rises shortly after six o'clock each morning and sets shortly before seven o'clock each evening. The effects of climate on plant life are well recognized, and even these relatively slight variations in daylight are critically important to farming. Tropical plants are apparently more sensitive to even slight changes in light, so that horticultural schedules must be followed rigorously. For example, rice planted too late in the year, i.e., after October, will almost certainly be smaller and imperfectly hardened.

The photosensitivity of tropical plants such as rice, and the factors of differences in length of day and amount of solar radiation because of clouds, have served to influence the temporal markers of the Iban year. The Iban contend that plants are sensitive not only to sunlight but also to differences in moonlight, and their "moon lore" is remarkably similar to the folklore of my native Alabama and other parts of the Southeastern United States. Thus, grains and other plants whose fruit grow above ground must be planted in the waxing of the moon, while tubers and plants producing below ground are planted when the moon is waning. Reference to the moon, Pleiades, Orion, and Sirius have helped the Iban take advantage of optimal growing conditions, i.e., the period when the greatest amount of moisture *and* light are available.

It is impossible to characterize easily the distribution of rainfall throughout the year. Available data reveal an erratic picture over the state, and figures for Sibu from the years 1915 to 1957 (Scott, 1964: 4) appear in Figure 2. According to Scott's summary, the average rainfall over the forty-two year period was 126.13 inches annually.

On the average, the wettest month is January with over thirteen inches of rain, and the driest month is June with seven and one-half inches. On average, more than ten inches of rain fall in every month between September and April. Monthly averages oversimplify the picture, however, as Figure 2 indicates. The dry season fails to develop in some areas, and during the usually wettest months of January and February less than five inches of rainfall have been recorded. When rain fell continuously for two weeks in February 1971, the people of Rumah Imba and Rumah Nyelang could not use the Durin Road—on which they have become dependent—to get rice when their supplies ran out. In some places the mud was up to fifteen inches deep.

On the basis of monthly rainfall, the year may be divided into two major seasons, with two shorter transitional periods. These seasons vary according to the location of the state and are more clearly distinguished on the coastal areas than in the interior.

The first season begins in April and lasts until July or August. This is the time of the southwest monsoon, marked by southwesterly winds and lower rainfall. During this season occurs the relatively short dry period (*musin kamarau*) of from one to four weeks that is utterly crucial to shifting cultivators. When the dry season fails to develop, cuttings from cleared fields remain wet and the firing of the fields is unsuccessful, so that plants and insects remain to damage the young rice, and crops are severely jeopardized.

The second season begins in October and lasts until February. During this wet season (*musin landas*) Sarawak is affected by the northeast monsoon, characterized by generally persistent and stronger northeasterly winds. This is the season when the heaviest rains fall, and when flooding is most apt to occur. Waters rise to flood level in upland areas as continuously heavy rainfall is funneled into the narrow gorges. Rising rapidly, rivers

Figure 2. Average and extreme monthly rainfall (1915–1957) at Sibu.

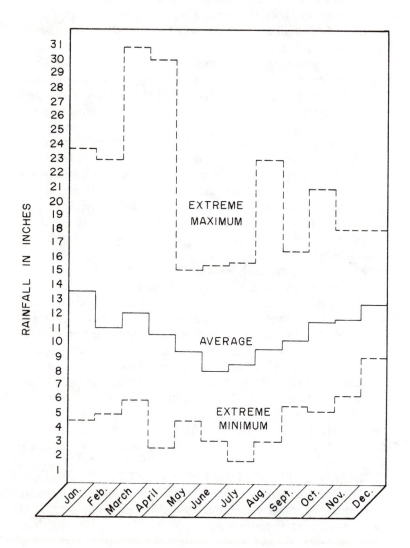

sometimes sweep away parts of or entire longhouses, as happened in the upper Menuan in 1970. In lowland areas, floodwaters spread over the plains for miles to a depth of three feet or more when rain-swollen rivers meet high tides.

Parenthetically, Iban longhouses traditionally have been built facing the water. It would be offensive as well as indiscreet to turn a community's back to a stream or river, for to do so would be an insult to Segundi', the god who created water.

The unpredictable nature of the two principal seasons is among the many imponderables that afflict the Iban cultivator. Not only does the dry season fail to develop in some years, but in others—for example 1972—an extended dry season may follow the sowing of the rice seed in the hills, and the young plants, requiring moisture, are damaged. In some years it is the wet season which develops late, and extreme values of thirty inches of rainfall have been recorded in both March and April. Such a late development may have disastrous results on rice crops. In the hills, heavy rains may shatter the panicles or pound the maturing grain into the mud. On the plains, mature rice may be spoiled by flooding.

The importance of the indeterminable rainfall is impossible to exaggerate in the adaptive practices of the Iban. A successful crop depends on close timing, optimal rainfall conditions, and the farmer's ability to read the signs. The Iban have developed their comprehensive rituals—in part scientific, recognizing the necessity of synchronizing farming activities with the most fortuitous natural conditions, and in part magical, attempting to control forces beyond human prediction—as a response to the vagaries of nature.

SOILS

Climate is important not only in terms of seasonal changes but also in its influence on soil formation. Throughout the world the nature of soils and the uses to which they can be put are determined to a great extent by climate. Many features of the soils of Sarawak are common to other parts of the humid tropics.

A major problem of soil fertility in the tropics is leaching. Leaching occurs when rainfall exceeds evaporation and results in a downward movement of water in the soil. Plant food, in the form of soluble silica and alumina, is carried downward leaving the insoluble sesquioxides of aluminum and iron on the surface. This means that the inorganic soil nutrients necessary to plant growth are seriously depleted because they are moved below the reach of plant roots.

A related problem is erosion. Erosion is influenced by the amount and intensity of rainfall, the topography of the land, vegetative cover, and the physical properties of the soil. While erosion is minimal in tropical lands under forest, it becomes a major problem to the farmer when the forest cover is removed and soils are exposed.

These two problems have combined to restrict the zones where farming can be practiced. In upland areas, leaching has accelerated the weathering of soils, and humus-poor, gray-white podzols and yellow clays predominate. In lowland areas, peat swamps consisting of as much as ninety feet of fibrous, undecomposed wood and leaves have been built up by erosion.

Contrary to the opinion that tropical soils are uniformly rich because they support luxuriant vegetation, great differences exist between soil types. Virgin forests, alluvium-enriched promontories, and a few pockets of igneous rock comprise sites of greatest fertility. While an American agronomist's calculation that "the Iowa farmer who owns two hundred acres of fertile land has more than is in all of Sarawak" is in error, much of the soil of the state is of low fertility or is quickly rendered thus after it has been cleared.

VEGETATION

Borneo is well named "the evergreen island." The combination of consistently warm temperatures and high relative humidity promote the plant growth that blankets much of the island. Despite extensive logging operations over the past twenty-five years, three-quarters of Sarawak is still covered by primary forest. Seen from the air, the trees appear to form a continuous carpet only occasionally showing signs of human activity.

At the highest levels are montane forests of oaks, chestnuts, and conifers. Because of the relative inaccessibility of these forests they remain intact.

Below these forests are hill dipterocarps which increase in number below 4,000 feet. These give way at 1,500 feet to the lowland dipterocarps which predominate from the foothills to the coastal plain. The lowland dipterocarps are dense, lofty, and unbranched below a canopy that is usually 150 feet or so above the ground. There is little ground growth because of the poor light, except for lianas and rattans that wander over the trees' high trunks. The dipterocarps constitute an ecological climax and stand on a shallow layer of soil enriched by leaves, branches, and other vegetation which is rapidly decomposed and recycled as plant food. Travel in primary forests is easy and pleasant since the ground is uncluttered with plants and the forests provide continuous shade. By contrast, travel through secondary forests may be difficult if not downright unpleasant because progress is impeded by all sorts of plants and the shade is not nearly so continuous.

The forests contain other hardwoods and some softwoods. There are several species of palms, including the coconut, *nipa, nibong,* areca, and sago. Other trees, ferns, and rattans have provided fruits and articles of commercial value supplied by the natives to traders. Para rubber (*Hevea brasiliensis*), introduced into the state at the end of the nineteenth century, is beyond question the most important of the non-native plants.

FAUNA

The fauna of Sarawak includes a wide variety. Banks (1949) discusses animals of 21 genera, together with sketches of lesser-known species that are unique to Borneo. Numerous primates include tree shrews, macaques, lorises, tarsiers, proboscis monkeys, gibbons, and orangutans. The only known nest-building bear in the world lives along the outer perimeter of the coastal plain and provides an interesting example of parallel development (cf. Schaller, 1964: 196–97). Wild pigs, deer, and anteaters live in the forests, though their numbers have been drastically reduced in the more densely populated lowland areas.

Smythies (1960) lists more than 200 species of birds found on the island. Some species are found on the coasts, others in the interior. An important aspect of the birds' presence is that there are no seasons when they are absent. Implications for rice farmers are obvious. Chickens are the most important domesticated fowl, though geese and ducks also are kept. Roosters are prized for cockfighting, while other chickens provide a major source of meat for ceremonial occasions.

The brahminy kite and seven other birds have been selected as the birds of omen in the elaborate Iban augury system. We shall discuss this later; suffice it to note here that augury has provided the Iban with a theologically important view of the world, through which the Iban have maintained belief in revelations which have been made to them but not to other societies.

The streams and rivers generally contain a rich aquatic life, including numerous species of fish, snails, and shrimp. The presence of the different species is dependent upon water conditions, and the techniques which the Iban have developed—use of fish traps, casting nets, hook-and-line—are adjusted according to the conditions.

There is a general adequacy of aquatic life in more remote areas, but in some parts of Sarawak, particularly in the lower parts of valleys and the lowlands generally, there has occurred a decimation of all riverine species as a result of overexploitation by the growing population or too frequent and liberal use of the derris root, which stuns larger fish and kills smaller ones. In those places where this has occurred, the result has been a shortage of this principal source of nonvegetable protein, or has been compensated for by the Iban's digging fish ponds or buying fish or meat from local shops.

Reptiles native to Sarawak include snakes, lizards, crocodiles, and turtles. There are only three poisonous snakes: the cobra, krait, and adder. Despite notions to the contrary, deaths due to snakebite are rare (Crisology, 1970). My wife had the unpleasant experience of having a cobra, probably exhausted from its swim, try to board our boat when we were tied up at the riverbank above Kapit. Leaping quickly to the other side of the boat, she raised the gunwales, preventing the snake from getting into the boat.

Subspecies of python include the reticulated python (*sawa'*) and Python curtus (*ripong*). Both are prized for their meat, which—like other snakes and the monitor lizard—is said to taste like chicken. I once observed the fileting of an eleven-foot reticulated python in Rumah Gaong. The snake had attacked a large sow whose squeals had attracted her owners. The Iban decapitated the snake and carried it onto the verandah where members of the longhouse gathered to share the meat.

Lizards range from four-inch house lizards, which help control insects, to the larger geckos, to monitor lizards. Monitor lizards are reputed to be scavengers, but they have been known to raid chicken houses. This seems plausible because the monitor lizards I have seen in Sibu have been swimming in the monsoon drain near the Malay cemetery. Paddling down the Pasai River at dusk one evening, two Iban and I surprised a four-foot lizard at the water's edge and it scurried back into the forest. This sighting elicited a number of stories about the lizards, ending with one from our prowsman who said that he had eaten monitor lizards until he once found matted hair and fingernails inside of one, proving to him that there was truth to stories about the lizards eating corpses.

Crocodiles are the largest of the reptiles. Along with the monitor lizards and other animals, they have retreated steadily before the advancing human settlements.

Insects abound in Sarawak. Secondary jungles especially are filled with the cacophony of the myriad tiny creatures. Ants, mosquitoes, houseflies, sandflies, horseflies, grasshoppers, cicadas, and other insects are important in natural processes and are less of a nuisance to the local human population than might be imagined. Other than insect-borne diseases, such as malaria, typhoid, dengue, and various gastrointestinal illnesses, the most serious problems are posed by damage to farms from insects such as the stem-borer and leaf-folder.

This discussion of the physical setting of Sarawak has not been meant to serve as an exhaustive account of the geography, botany, and zoology of that state. Readers interested in further information in these areas are encouraged to read Allen (1970), Banks (1949), Browne (1955), Jackson (1968), Lee (1970), Parsons (1966), and pertinent articles in the *Sarawak Museum Journal*. The attempt in this chapter has been to present schematically the most salient features of the environment in which the Iban, insofar as they are known historically, have created their world.

Chapter 2

MIGRATIONS AND THEIR CAUSES

The world of the Iban has undergone changes not only because of contacts with people from abroad, but also because of internal movements into new settings. Early accounts indicate that the Iban traditionally have been a very mobile people. During the past millenium their ancestors moved northward through Kalimantan. Two centuries ago they entered Sarawak from the south. Since that time they have spread across Sarawak and into the adjoining states of Brunei and Sabah.

Many details of these movements are unknown. Few accounts prior to the nineteenth century exist and those that do are, for the most part, impressionistic and based upon limited contacts with the Iban. More reliable reporting begins in the mid-nineteenth century. From these records, from the oral traditions of the Iban, and through a knowledge of the natural conditions to which the Iban adapted, it is possible for us to describe the factors which have contributed to Iban mobility and to analyze this behavioral norm for its importance in the changing world of the Iban.

ECOLOGICAL FACTORS

The abundance of plant and animal life, together with the continuing importance of nonhorticultural activities, made movements into new areas attractive in aboriginal times. Older

Iban still recount wistfully their movements into valleys where "plants were plentiful, streams filled with fish, and the forests teeming with wild pigs and deer." (While memories play tricks, an important feature of Iban wanderlust has been the conviction—expressed here in retrospect—that a better life awaited them "out there.")

The technology of the Iban, limited to simple tools and human energy, made continuation of so-called subsidiary activities essential. Unable to produce enough food on their farms, they had to continue to get food in other ways. Gathering wild vegetables, fishing, hunting, and cultivating tubers still account for up to 50 percent of the foodstuffs of Iban in remote areas, i.e., places where they are unable to trade for food. In my sample of longhouses whose members predominantly farm hill rice, only 10 percent of the families were self-sufficient in rice. At some time each year most families were forced to resort to nonhorticultural activities not merely to augment their staple food of rice but as a means of survival.

The Iban were fully aware of the resources of the forests for trade as well as for food (cf. Low, 1848). Contacts with Malays and Chinese stimulated an interest in trade for camphor, rattans, the natural rubbers gutta percha and india rubber, and the illipe nut. Expeditions into unpopulated areas provided opportunities to collect rhinoceros horns, which were famous for their aphrodisiac properties, kingfisher feathers, bezoar stones (calcified deposits found in the viscera of certain animals), and casques of the helmeted hornbill, once more valuable than jade.

Whereas techniques of collection made movements into new areas attractive, the development of techniques of food production and the concomitant growth of population made such movements imperative. The hilly soils which the Iban brought under cultivation made movements necessary because of the conditions discussed earlier. Removal of vegetation and the exposure of the soils to sunlight and hard rains resulted in structural and chemical changes within one or two years. The techniques of cultivation, involving rotation of fields, and the settlement patterns, involving frequent movements of people, reflect the awareness the Iban have of the fragile character of the soils and the delicately complex balance between soils, plant life, and man.

Like other shifting cultivators, the Iban have been accused of being padi-field profligates and wastrels, of leveling vast tracts of primary forest and leaving sedge deserts behind. While such criticisms are in part correct, they ignore factors which led to the development of shifting cultivation as a viable and defensible technology.

The hills of Sarawak are suitable for the extension of horticulture, but not for its intensification. There are few areas in the hilly zones with enough flat land to make intensive agriculture practicable. The gradient on most hillsides is too steep to permit terracing, and the few attempts to build terraces have resulted in landslides. The topsoil is too thin to warrant deep-plowing. Plowing would serve only to turn over the infertile subsoils. So the dibble stick, the tool of the shifting cultivator who punches holes in the soil that is to receive the seed, is an appropriate tool which permits sowing with only a minimum disturbance of the soil.

The Iban have been keen students of soils and are well aware of land-yield relations. They have been continually concerned about receiving maximum returns in harvests from their investments in energy and time, and are cognizant of the significant decrease in yields from fields cultivated for more than two years in succession.

Movements to new areas or to farms previously cultivated have been necessary to avoid overcultivation of the soils. New land may be cultivated for two years in succession, after which fallowing is absolutely necessary to avoid irreparable damage to the soil. Land farmed previously may be cultivated for one year, after which it must be fallowed from six to twelve years to avert soil damage and the invasion of *Imperata cylindrica,* the noxious grass whose rhizomes or underground shoots can reach nutrients which have been leached beyond the reach of rice roots. Overcultivation of hill farms and the spread of *Imperata cylindrica* have created vast "green deserts" in Sarawak, and such deserts cover millions of acres throughout Southeast Asia.

The Iban have maintained a low density of population by the periodic hiving off of small groups. Some Iban have remained in the hills while the larger group passed through, moving into new areas. As a result, the Iban population of the Second Division of Sarawak has remained surprisingly constant over the past century-and-a-quarter in contrast to the growth of the Iban population in the Third through the Seventh Divisions. (Sarawak is divided into seven divisions, similar to counties in the United States, with administrative, health, educational, police, and other divisional headquarters in each. Each division is further divided into districts.) Just prior to 1850 the Iban of the Second Division were estimated to number about 50,000. The census of 1960 showed an Iban population of 70,634 in that division, a figure which is lower than might be expected from an average annual increase among the Iban of 1.7 percent. This constancy is to be explained by movement of Iban from the Second Division northward and eastward.

Shifting cultivation was possible because of the low population density also in the areas into which Iban have moved. Even today upland regions of Borneo are sparsely populated. The density of the newly formed Seventh Division of Sarawak, for instance, is only 3.5 persons per square mile.

Not all movements of Iban into new places can be construed in positive terms, such as having taken place because of attractions of forest products or predilection for virgin land. Some moves were made reluctantly, with accompanying hardships. The clearing of enough new land to make a farm is beyond the capability of the labor force of the average Iban family. Therefore, most movements involved more than one family to provide for labor exchange. In places where the Iban had farmed, previously cultivated land could be used in conjunction with farms cut into the forests. In new areas, however, the Iban were dependent upon the land that could be cleared prior to the dry season. It is understandable, therefore, why the Iban have cleared their farms imperfectly—not only is such clearing a means of reducing erosion, but it is also less demanding on the limited labor force.

Although the carrying capacity of lands in Sarawak varies greatly, and while it is doubtful if any rural areas approach overpopulation, the Iban have been a litigious people where land has been concerned, and doubtlessly many movements have occurred to resolve conflicts. Calculations of carrying capacity and optimal population are always difficult to determine and almost always neglect basic considerations such as culturally perceived pressures on land.

Perceived pressures have stemmed from the Iban's recognition that some land, such as the montane region, is virtually inaccessible, while other land, such as the swamps, is unproductive, thus leading to a high evaluation of fertile soil. Despite the eagerness with which the Iban have attacked forests on new sites, the clearing of the land has been an arduous task and the Iban have placed a premium upon *cleared* productive land, as reflected in the traditional land tenure system. Pioneers who felled primary forests for farming thereby established their rights and those of their descendants to cleared land in perpetuity. Boundaries were marked by bamboo rows planted along property lines. Rights to land were transmitted orally in lengthy genealogies. And the longhouse functioned—and continues to function—as an indigenous land office, as disputes between members of the same community or of different longhouses could be judged by those persons most knowledgeable about earlier settlements.

Although population density has been low, the Iban have been a litigious people, especially when cleared land has been involved. Spencer St. John, British Consul in Brunei, wrote shortly after the mid-nineteenth century that disputes over land were the principal factor in intrafamilial disagreements (St. John, 1862: I: 50). Reports of such disputes are numerous in the records of Residents of the Second Division into the early twentieth century.

Next we shall examine the institutionalized responses of the Iban to the natural conditions we have noted, and to the presence of other indigenous groups.

CULTURAL FACTORS

The world of the Iban has been created not only from the interplay of men with nature, but also from interpersonal relations between Iban and others. Living among other native groups—some of them hunter-gatherers such as the Ukits and Punans, others farmers such as the Bidayuh, Melanau, Kayan, and Kenyah—the Iban have been involved in a contest for land.

This contest took place not because other land was unavailable, but rather because members of other groups often hunted or occupied areas which the Iban found desirable for rice cultivation. In some cases the Iban forcefully drove out the other groups, as in their invasions of territories occupied by Melanau, Ukits, Kayans, and Sians. In other instances the Iban formed alliances with members of other groups, as with the Bukitan who served as guides to the Iban, leading them into new areas, eventually themselves adopting rice farming and longhouse organization. In still other cases, members of other groups were captured and assimilated as slaves in Iban society.

Historically, the Iban have held an edge over other indigenous groups in aggression and achievement orientation. Selection of these behavioral norms probably was related to the Iban determination to farm what appeared to them to be the best soils, and was reinforced with myth and ritual by which other groups were pitted against the Iban.

Evidence is inconclusive, but the Iban may have enjoyed an edge in weaponry over other groups. (For a similar situation in Venezuela see Chagnon, 1974: 8–11.) The use of iron appears to be of considerable historical depth, evidenced by the universal use of piston bellows and the common knowledge of smithing among Iban males. Trade on the coast provided iron in exchange for forest products. Acquisition of iron was also related to the expansionist ardor which the Iban have shown.

In aboriginal Iban society, where all members were potentially equal, incentives for achievement were provided by the development of statuses of prestige. While these statuses were appeals to the self-interest of the individual, they also served the collective interest of the group.

Freeman is quite correct in describing the Iban as egalitarian and classless (1970). Nevertheless, sharing what Claude Lévi-Strauss has called the "original human logic" for comparing and contrasting even the slightest of differences, the Iban have judged the performances of individuals and have shown their evaluations in the honors accorded to or withheld from them. These honors, including preferential marriages for one's children, seats of honor, and requests from others for blessings on festive occasions, have spurred Iban on to a series of outstanding actions.

Culturally defined ways to prestige have been clearly prescribed. The first step to upward mobility was in pioneering. The pioneer not only contributed to the survival of the Iban by opening up new land, but also obtained distinction for himself and his descendants. Kinsmen of pioneers frequently formed the core of alliances around which communities formed. Thus, for example, the community at Rumah Nyala still recalls three brothers who originally moved to the Aup area; the descendants of these brothers occupy the centralmost units of the longhouse, a structural expression of their positions vis-à-vis other residents, and the present headman of the house reckons his descent from the pioneers.

The second step towards a higher status was continuously successful farming. With the beginning of rice cultivation, the Iban invested a considerable part of their efforts in farming. Although subsidiary activities continued to be important, rice became synonymous with food, other plants and meat being considered as condiments. Thus, crop failures were a serious threat, both nutritionally and to the self-image of the Iban. A bountiful harvest, on the other hand, was evidence of the farmer's ability and divine favor.

Success in rice farming has been described by Iban as the *sine qua non* for prestige. Those farmers who were famous for their successes in the fields were invited to horticultural festivals at which they pronounced blessings on the sponsors and other guests so that the latter might share their good fortune. The successful farmer laid by a supply of rice that hopefully was adequate for both his family and his less able kinsmen and friends. Those who produced surpluses loaned rice to their more unfortunate neighbors who, in addition to being indebted and placed in a dependent position, repaid the loans in rice, game, fish, labor, or forest produce, thus further strengthening the position of the more able farmers.

It is my observation—and interviews confirm this—that the fortunes of most Iban farmers have generally been unpredictable. A majority of Iban have faced periodic shortages, a time commonly referred to as the "month(s) when the ladle hangs empty." In some years supplies have been exhausted long before the new harvest and families have been forced to borrow from others or subsist on other foods.

A few farmers have been notoriously unsuccessful, due either to their own ineptness or to real misfortune. Whatever the cause, as one bad harvest followed another they became recognized as either incompetent or as victims of divine displeasure. Members of such families sometimes became irrevocably indebted to more successful farmers and, lacking altogether any hope of repaying their creditors, they ultimately became attached to the families who supplied their food.

Ecological and cultural demands for success and the accompanying penalties of failure made rice farming the canon by which families were judged. Positions within this world accrued to individuals and families according to whether they pioneered or followed, and especially according to whether they were capable farmers.

Most Iban families had both good years and bad years, and were able to subsist largely through their own efforts. Such families formed the largest part of Iban society and are known today as "commoners" or "most people" *(mensia mayoh),* or "the thousands" *(mensia saribu).* These families occupy a middle-range status.

The lowest status to which Iban might fall in the traditional society was that of the debt slave. "Durian seed slaves" *(ulun leka rian),* as they were called, were those who suffered successive crop failure. The term by which they came to be called indicated that they were willing to eat whatever they could get. This group occupied a detested place because they and their descendants were said to be permanently bound to their "owners." (One prominent Iban, educated in the United States, told me that he still has claim to ten families who are descendants of his ancestors' slaves.) Unlike slaves captured in raids who might be adopted into their captor's family, debt slaves were not redeemed. Because of their misfortunes, other families did not want their children to marry descendants of debt slaves.

The highest position in Iban society was that of the *raja berani,* or "courageous wealthy." This position—the significance of which and the steps leading to its acquisition were analyzed for me by Mr. Benedict Sandin, former curator of the Sarawak Museum and foremost student of Iban folklore—was open to all males. Only a few, however, were able to combine the three requirements of pioneering, successful farming, and war-leader. Those few who did are remembered as idealized personalities, and are immortalized as central characters in history through which the widely scattered Iban still relate to one another.

In addition to the obligations previously discussed, the position of *raja berani* required that its holder demonstrate his courage by taking a human head. Headhunting, like pioneering, was related to the expansion of Iban into new areas. Without implying any causal relationship, headhunting and shifting cultivation proceeded together, "blade-in-hand." Parallels between the two institutions appear in a number of plays-on-words, as in the reference to felling trees and men, and of "harvesting" the heads of rice and men.

Headhunting was a complex institution with a variety of themes and values. The primary function of headhunting, in addition to providing a means for showing one's courage, was the integration of opposing elements in the Iban world. Together with the familiar coordinates of male-female, sun-moon, and good-evil, the Iban also divided their world into states of *dunya*, "here and now," and *sebayan*, "the opposite." *Dunya* is the land of the living, the known, where behavior is regulated according to positive and negative sanctions. *Sebayan* is the land of the "dead," not in the English sense of the word, but literally of the "opposite of living," the unknown, where anything goes. All that is proscribed in *dunya* is permitted in *sebayan*. What cannot happen in *dunya* happens in *sebayan*.

Headhunting received its mythical charter when the spirit Puntang Raga' (literally "The Breakthrough") directed a culture hero, Serapoh, to bury the dead. Until that time corpses had been left unattended where they fell. (This mythical account of a time when there were no practices of burial and no rituals of the dead is fascinating, because such practices presumably have existed in all societies from the time of *Homo sapiens neandertalensis* or from 150,000 B.P. Harrison's [1974] report of a similar absence of burial practices among the Ranau Dusun, however, lends credibility to the tradition.) In addition to directing Serapoh to bury the dead, Puntang Raga' also instructed him to institute a period of mourning for the deceased who could be released from *dunya* and move on to *sebayan* only by the taking of a human head.

The transformations which headhunting thus effected are four fold. At a basic level, the death of an enemy whose head was taken helped maintain a balance between opposed units.

Second, the "head" replaced the "life" of the deceased. Third, the "capture" of the head ensured the "release" of the deceased. As the head was brought in, the deceased moved out. Finally, as the deceased entered *sebayan,* he bridged "the opposite state" and "here and now," taking the first step in the metamorphosis of man into dew for the nourishment of rice for the nourishment of man, and so on.

Headhunting also served to integrate symbolically opposed social units. The Iban have conceptualized their world as consisting of a series of roughly concentric circles (see Figure 3, page 38). The primary unit was the family, the next a core of kinsmen, third the longhouse community, then an alliance group, beyond that the Iban, and finally "others." Within each circle the principle of interaction was reciprocity; beyond each circle the expectation was exploitation.

The Iban have seen themselves as a distinctly human group and, like numerous other people, have attempted to put distance between themselves and other groups through the use of animal epithets. Dehumanization is, of course, not peculiar to the Iban. Although we often are unaware of our own dehumanizing attitudes and actions, we attempt to place individuals and groups who are different from us into other-than-human categories by applying to them such terms as "pig," "dog," "ass," "skunk," "snake," "ape," "monkey," "cat," and "bird." Thus, Malays were referred to as "pig's snout" *(junggur)* because of their Islamic prohibitions on pork. After the Second World War, during which some Chinese collaborated with the Japanese, the Chinese of Sarawak were called "the Japanese mousedeer" *(pelandok Jipun).* Euro-Americans are called "white pigs" *(babi belang)* and "white chickens" *(manok labang)* because of their size and color.

In fairness to the Iban it must be noted that in their folk literature they symbolize themselves as well as other groups in animal categories. However, more often than not the slow-moving tortoise and the diminutive mousedeer, favorite symbols of the Iban in such delightfully poignant folk-stories as "The Animals Fish with Derris" *(Jelu Nubai)* and "The Mousedeer and the Leopard" *(Pelandok enggau Remaung),* emerge as heroes and the other animals as clods.

The significance of this is that by application of non-human symbols to members of other groups, the Iban have placed them in the category of the exploitable. Like trees in a new forest, non-Iban were there for the felling. Like new land, other groups existed to receive the implantation of Iban. Like game, members of other people were there for the hunting.

Despite the use of animal epithets, however, *other* people are not *other* animals. No matter how agile the mental gymnastics to rationalize aggressive actions against other groups, no matter how neat the categories into which they were placed, there remained an awareness among the Iban of the humanity of those people different from themselves. That this is not merely my speculation is apparent in the fact that the remains of animals were not accorded the same rites as were the remains of other-than-Iban persons, nor were animals assimilated into Iban society.

Headhunting, thus, was rationalized in terms of an extension of the final circle—the Iban—to include former non-human enemies. The victim died to old relationships but was born into new ones. The ritual activities associated with headhunting illustrate how enmity was transformed into friendship. After the head of an enemy had been taken, it was ceremonially received at the foot of the longhouse ladder, just as is a guest at a festival. Women of the house acclaimed over the head. After the skull had been cleaned, it was hung in a wicker casing in a place of prominence on the verandah of the head-taker's family, as testimony to the courage of the hunter and in honor of the spirit of the skull. The skull was thought to be capable of sentient action. Neglect of it—as of any Iban—would result in some community calamity. To avert such misfortune fires were lit on ceremonial occasions beneath the skull, and it was "fed" as rice was smeared on its jaws.

Headhunting "at-oned" hunter and victim, Iban and other. Previously the enemy had been "out there"; his skull was brought "in here" for the mutual good of his spirit and his host. Just as the hunter was expected to feed the skull, so, too, the spirit of the skull was expected to act beneficently on behalf of the hunter and his family.

Although headhunting permitted the symbolic extension of social boundaries, these boundaries were physically extended by the assimilation of members of other groups. An examination of historical documents and numerous conversations with Iban have led me to conclude that, despite the importance of head-hunting and the ramifying rituals, the number of persons decapitated was small in comparison to the number of captives. Without doubt there were notable headhunters, such as the late Penghulu Gani of Bawang Assan, an acquaintance of mine, who had twenty-six heads to his credit, and whose death was appropriately noted in Associated Press releases. But the number of heads taken was small when contrasted to the remarkable growth of the Iban, a feat accomplished through the capture and assimilation of non-Iban.

The enslavement of captives was a most desirable alternative to headhunting. Headhunting was a terror tactic designed to drive other groups from their territories; capture and redemption was a technique for swelling Iban forces. Skulls might give spiritual aid, but captives could work, and through redemption fight alongside their new kinsmen.

Redemption was the institutionalized means by which non-Iban became Iban. Slaves of the brave (*ulun berani,* a much less despised degree of slavery than the "durian seed slave") lived with the families of their captors. Those deemed worthy were brought before the longhouse community where the captor declared his intention to take the captive as a brother/sister. Before the assembly, the captive was given objects marking his passage from the former status to Iban commoner—axe, bush-knife, gong, jar, and rice. Following the ritual, any Iban who referred to the redeemed person as a slave was subject to a fine.

It is ironic that raiding, particularly for the purpose of as-similating non-Iban, actually compounded the problem of population distribution and contributed directly to the necessity of Iban mobility. For as new captives were taken and the population grew, so too did pressures—real and perceived—on land. As we have seen, the Iban response was to leave a portion of the community behind while others engaged in new invasions, new contests for land, and the enlargement of the Iban world.

COLONIAL RULE

Push came to shove, and Iban migrations grew larger due to conflicts stemming from the imposition of colonial rule on Sarawak. Movements of Iban into the Rejang Valley have been described by historians of Sarawak (cf. Pringle, 1970) as the most important events of the nineteenth century. These movements were in no small measure a response to the British presence and what the Iban considered to be interference with their ways of life.

The arrival of James Brooke in Sarawak in 1841 and the establishment of the Brooke Raj inevitably led to changes among the people of Sarawak. Upon his agreement to help the Malay Sultan of Brunei suppress piracy and raiding, Brooke was recognized as Rajah by the Sultan. Brooke and his heirs expanded their authority over what is the present-day state of Sarawak.

The Brookes attempted to restrict Iban movements and headhunting, and to strengthen their rule by levying taxes on the native population. The Iban responses varied. Some viewed Brooke and his family as a threat to Iban mobility and independence and reacted with the time-honored alternatives of fight and flight. Other Iban saw in the Brookes an opportunity for personal advantage by allying themselves with the technologically superior British.

Whether the Iban reacted by fighting the Brookes or by aligning themselves with the Raj, the growth of this foreign administration in Sarawak had fundamental and irrevocable consequences in their lives. Quite literally, the old heaven and earth passed away, and a new world emerged whose center was no longer the longhouse but the town, the capital, London, *menoa tasik,* "lands beyond the sea."

Paradoxically, the unity of Iban society derived from its factionalism. New units were generated from the dialectic of previously opposed ones. The image I hold of the pre-Brooke Iban is of a dynamic society, producing hardy leaders who rallied their followers with or against their counterparts.

The unity of Iban society, in addition to use of a common language and other symbols, was focused upon a host of culture heroes. These culture heroes provided examples for behavior. As semidivine beings they shone in the Iban sky. Myths about the heroes grew as tomorrow's god was born out of today's *raja berani.*

The *raja berani* share numerous similarities with the so-called Big Man (cf. Sahlins, 1963) of Melanesia. As we have discussed, the *raja berani* were consummate individuals combining the foremost values of masculinity—pioneering, success in farming, and raiding. The *raja berani,* however, was no stronger than the faction he could build through his own achievements. Verbally persuasive, the *raja berani* were highly competitive, undercutting rivals and stealing their followers. The indicative quality of the *raja berani* was personal power, evidence of a peculiar relationship with the supernatural in life and into which the *raja berani* moved at death.

Therefore, the *raja berani* must be recognized as more than self-aggrandizing individuals, which, admittedly, they were too. They were more than erstwhile political leaders, though they were that as well. The *raja berani* were nodes to which were attached the various strands of Iban society, the result being a loosely woven cultural fabric transcending time and space.

The demise of the *raja berani* has had more than mere political implications, however. Several years ago an Iban brought to us a box filled with carvings of the god of fertility, Sempulang Gana. "We no longer have any gods in whom we can believe," he explained. "Our gods are now in the government offices." The twilight of their gods began for the Iban with the coming of the Brookes; though some remain, they now coexist with foreign divinities who often eclipse them in importance.

The Brookes became *Raja Berani* among *raja berani.* Whereas previously the Iban had been a dominant people vis-à-vis other Bornean groups, they were placed in a position subordinate to the Brookes. The reactions of Iban factions were various, but for all of them there occurred a shift in the locus of power as a result of which the Iban world was turned inside out. Heretofore the Iban perceived themselves as living in the center of their universe; following the imposition of colonial rule they felt themselves moved to the perimeter.

Brooke policies of taxation and fines, restrictions on movements, and suppression of headhunting and raiding led some *raja berani* and their factions to rebel. As an example of this reaction and its consequences we shall examine the story of Lintong. Lintong was a leader who adamantly refused to acknowledge the Brooke administration. He was annoyed by the Rajah's taxes and angered by fines imposed on two of his followers. A Lemanak Iban who had migrated to the Julau River,

Lintong was urged by his brother, Buah Raya, to pay the tax of one dollar a year "because we now are held by the Rajah." Lintong refused, arguing that he still led his people and that he had made no agreement to pay anything to the Rajah.

In an attempt to restrict migrations, the Brookes built a system of forts which commanded the key points along the main rivers of Sarawak. Fort Brooke was built on Sibu Island in 1862, and shortly after its completion, Lintong made preparations to attack the fort and take the heads of the staff. Lintong's raid on the fort with "three thousand men" (Ranee Margaret, 1913: 35) failed, and his party withdrew up the Kanowit River.

Slyly letting it be known that he planned another attack, Lintong had his men build a new and now legendary boat, *Bung Ungkap,* which was equipped with saplings lashed across the bow and tied back on both sides of the boat. When cut, the saplings would snap forward, slashing through the boatloads of the Rajah's forces when they were encountered. The ensuing battle was short-lived, however, for Lintong's forces could not withstand the Rajah's troops who were armed with guns and small cannons. A cannon shot sank the boat—which later rose from the water as a mythical python *(nabau)* of enormous size —and Lintong's followers were routed. (The *nabau* has figured prominently in the Iban "theology of hope." Though destroyed, *Bung Ungkap* arose in a more powerful form. The late Penghulu Gani is reported to have appeared on a jetty as an immense python, and similar tales are related about other *raja berani.)*

Shortly after the battle, Lintong sued for peace. In return for amnesty, the Rajah forced him to settle across the river from Fort Brooke in the Middle Rejang Valley.

Although some leaders such as Lintong were openly belligerent to the Brookes until forced to submit, others saw in the Rajahs an opportunity to confirm their positions by siding with the government against the rebels. Limited as they were in personnel and funds, the Rajahs took every advantage of strengthening ties between themselves and friendly Iban by making them part of punitive operations in which, interestingly, headhunting—otherwise illegal—was legitimized as a way of punishing dissidents. (In this way and in others the Brookes demonstrated their power by permitting to allies what they prohibited to enemies.)

Alliances with friendly Iban may be illustrated in the story of the second Rajah, Charles Brooke, and the famous leader Munan. The son of Minggat, himself a famous government war leader who engaged in many punitive campaigns against Iban rebels in the Upper Katibas and Lupar Rivers during the 1870s and 1880s, Munan became involved in a grand-scale feud over the appointment of a successor to his father as chief *(Penghulu)*. When another man was appointed to the chieftainship, Munan allegedly urged rebellion and was jailed. Released at the end of the summer of 1893, Munan was ordered to move to Sibu where he could be supervised by the staff of Fort Brooke.

After arriving in the Rejang Valley, Munan and his followers built a longhouse on Kerto Island opposite Sibu. Munan was a skillful politician. He secured his command of the Lower Rejang Valley by obtaining the Rajah's appointment of his kinsmen as chiefs in Sarikei, Bawang Assan, Aup, and Durin. With these alliances, Munan was at the center of such a military network that he became the most important figure for the Rajah's war expeditions in the Rejang Valley.

In 1900, Munan was accorded special recognition by the Rajah who conferred on him the unusual title *Penghulu Dalam,* or the "in/deep Penghulu," the one on whom the Rajah depended. He sat on the state's legislative council, the Council Negri, and received a regular salary from the government as a native magistrate empowered to hear cases in court.

Munan's story is important for several reasons. First, when he urged rebellion he wanted to *migrate* to the Rejang but was prevented by Brooke administrators. It is ample testimony to his political ability that, following his release from jail he was *forced to settle* in the Rejang—the place he originally had wanted to move to—a move reminiscent of the psychology used by Br'er Rabbit on his adversaries in "The Tar Baby" story.

Second, Munan is representative of the physically and culturally mobile Iban, whose proclivities for pioneering have been preadaptive in contact situations. Such Iban have been quick to seize upon acculturative experiences which they have judged to be advantageous. Munan was the first Iban in the Rejang Valley to plant rubber. So great was his success that the government sought his advice when it established a rubber estate near Kuching in 1903. He invested in shophouses in the town of Sibu, and following a fire which destroyed the market area in 1902 was the first businessman to undertake reconstruction of his shophouses. He also held rights to extensive tracts of land in the town. At the time of his passing he was beyond any question the most powerful Iban in the Rejang Valley.

SUMMARY

The history of Iban migrations is complex and at best a confused and incomplete picture. At the beginning of the nineteenth century the Iban were largely living in the upriver areas of the major rivers and their tributaries of the Second Division. They had moved into Sarawak from Kalimantan some time earlier. By 1850 the Iban had moved northward and reached the Rejang Valley.

The Iban migrations were not highly organized ventures involving hundreds of people. Rather they were the gradual, irregular movements of people who farmed, gathered, hunted, and then moved on, always on the lookout for new and potentially rewarding areas.

Iban migrations to the Rejang Valley coincided with the extension of Brooke rule and the arrival of other groups, most notably coastal Malays and immigrant Chinese. Out of the interplay between natural and social forces the world of the Iban has been formed and transformed. Just as they have been physically mobile, so too have the Iban been remarkably responsive to new circumstances, resulting to a reordering of their ways of life and view of the world.

Chapter 3

SOCIAL ORGANIZATION

The organizing principles of the Iban have developed as part of the strategies of adaptation in various settings. In the hills, where shifting cultivation of dry rice has been practiced, Iban residences traditionally were impermanent aggregates of small families which clustered together for food-sharing during times of seasonal scarcity and for purposes of defense against enemies.

Kinship has been the principal idiom by which people have related to one another. Longhouses have been organized around a core of kinsmen. Cooperative activities have been rationalized in terms of kin-ties. Non-kinsmen and even non-Iban have been assimilated through the creation of flexible networks of kinship. Manipulation of genealogies up to thirty generations in depth have allowed the Iban to travel to new areas with the confidence that they will certainly find "kinsmen" and, hence, hospitality—whether they actually know anyone or not.

We now shall examine the units that comprise Iban society. It is necessary to emphasize that these units reveal the same sort of flexibility that we have seen in Iban settlements. The units' boundaries are purposefully vague; thus each unit is permeable and individuals often change their membership. George Peter Murdock's comment that "social structures exist to be manipulated" is particularly relevant in the case of the Iban.

Figure 3. Units in Iban organization.

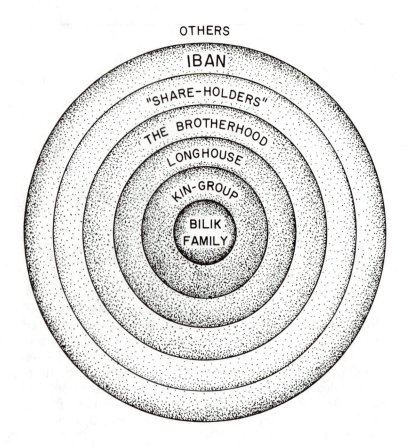

OTHERS

IBAN

"SHARE-HOLDERS"

THE BROTHERHOOD

LONGHOUSE

KIN-GROUP

BILIK
FAMILY

THE *BILIK*-FAMILY

The fundamental unit of Iban society is the *bilik*-family. The term *bilik* is taken from the name of the family room in the longhouse.

Subject as they have been to the vagaries of nature, the Iban have survived through cultural selection for opposed yet supportive families. Through an apparently relaxed yet intense stress upon individualism, the Iban have inculcated within their members such degrees of self-interest that adult siblings rarely are able to live together in the same quarters. Yet it is indicative of the thoroughgoing self-interest of the Iban that while he feels it to be to his advantage to "go it on his own," he is aware that there will be times when he requires help from his kin. Thus the Iban state that "we cannot live with each other, but it is certain that we could not live without each other."

The *bilik*-family is comprised in most cases of two or three generations. I analyzed 1,051 families over a ten-year period and found a predominance of the nuclear family—parents and their children—which occurred in 596 cases. Families including three generations were found in 400 cases. The average family includes between five and six persons.

The *bilik*-family is an autonomous unit, able to join with or detach from other units. In the words of Kudi, an elderly Iban from the Upper Rejang, "The *bilik*-family is like a sovereign state." This sense of autonomy is obviously supportive of the ideal of individualism.

The *bilik*-family is responsible for the production of its own food supply. Although it may exchange labor with members of other families, it still manages its own affairs, succeeding or failing largely on its own. In this respect, selection for the small family appears ecologically sound, for while some families may fail, hopefully others will have more success. And through the division of the producing units the Iban have avoided putting all their rice in one bin.

The *bilik*-family is defined primarily by the idiom of kinship and affinity. Iban relate to one another through either parent and through more distant kinsmen. Although local residence is an important criterion in the definition of family membership, it is by no means an exclusive one.

The *bilik*-family readily releases and readmits members, thus providing a high degree of personal mobility. Members leave and return according to personal advantages. It is my opinion that this fact has been psychologically important in pioneering activities, for the Iban leaves in the confidence that he will find kinsmen or a receptive family unit where he is going, and with the assurance that he will be able to return should it be necessary.

The *bilik*-family is a kin-based corporate group. To the Iban, a family endures over generations through the use of various symbols of continuity, such as the family's sacred rice (a strain selected in lieu of a surname), charms, and ritual prohibitions which are peculiar to and distinctive of each family. Each family enjoys rights to heirlooms and lands cleared by its ancestors. Time past and future meet in the symbols of family continuity which are shared by each new generation.

The *bilik*-family is a status-conferring group, a fact of significance in the ethnic evolution of the status-conscious Iban. Children traditionally have been named for a grandparent or great-grandparent, according to the sex of the child and in keeping with the concept of the cycle of life as human-dew-rice-human. In addition to reinforcing notions about the cyclical flow of life, naming has served two other functions. First, by naming a child for an ancestor the Iban identified the kin-group of the child, providing a means of distinguishing members of groups who were notoriously poor farmers or those who were said to be agents of evil and able to put a hex on people or plants. Second, naming children for ancestors implemented the Iban desire for mnemonic immortality, ensuring that the ancestor would be remembered in his namesake. Among the mobile Iban, a grave might be forgotten in rapidly growing jungles, and a living namesake was more desirable than a quickly rotted wooden marker.

Recruitment to the *Bilik*-Family

There are four means by which Iban become members of a family: birth, adoption, marriage, and incorporation.

Each child at birth becomes a member of his father's and mother's family, assuming that they have not divorced prior to his birth. Final responsibility for the nurture and education of the child rests with his family of birth. By virtue of his birth into the family, the child acquires equal rights to the family's property—as long as he remains a member of that family.

Children are highly desired and prized, both as objects and givers of affection, as well as for the valuable labor resource they represent. The Iban are nothing if not pragmatic about their children. Upon the death of a teenaged youngster, I overheard a woman bemoan the fact that the parents had invested so much in the child but would receive nothing in return.

Children represent potential security. In the words of one woman:

We covet many children, the more the better. A single child is like a fishhook with only one barb; if it snaps, the fish is gone. We fish with a three-barbed hook, and the least number of children we want is three.

Membership in the family is limited according to the local residence of a child's parents. He may be a member of his parents' family if they are living by themselves, or he may be a member of his maternal or paternal grandparents' family if his parents live with one of their families.

While a child is born into only one family, by birth he becomes a member of both his father's and his mother's kin-groups (suku juru, kaban belayan). Although he may never have need to activate these ties, members of these kin-groups are potentially important for support and aid. These relations are acknowledged symbolically by token gifts of salt, ginger, or chilis—that the child's speech may be powerful and well-seasoned—from his kinsmen upon the child's first visit to their bilik.

A second way by which membership in the family is achieved is through adoption. Adoption has been a fairly common practice among the Iban for four reasons. First, while marriage is almost universal, there has been a high rate of childlessness. Being without children is a source of shame and practical concern, and it is understandable why the Iban have looked upon barrenness (punas) as a curse. Many Iban women have been childless because of dietary problems. Some have miscarried because of excessively heavy work or inadequate antenatal care. Some have aborted lest their husbands lose interest in them and look elsewhere for sexual pleasure. Others deliver successfully, but practices such as cutting the umbilical cord with a bamboo sliver and rubbing ash from the hearth into the child's navel have resulted in a high incidence of tetanus. These practices, together with postpartum taboos restricting the mother's diet to rice and salt for one month following her delivery, account for the infant mortality rate which ranged from 40 to 51 percent in the longhouses I surveyed.

A second reason for the practice of adoption has been the traditional system of social security. Oriented as they have been to a technology based upon the collection and cultivation of perishable items, and simply unable to "lay by for old age," the Iban have developed a cardinal rule of residence to ensure care for the aged; viz., one child must remain in the family of birth to care for his parents. Childless parents anticipating the time when they no longer can farm and produce enough food for their survival adopt a child to care for them. The adopted child becomes heir or heiress in the family, maintains the *bilik*'s continuity over time, and performs the rituals required by the parents at the time of and following their deaths. The adoptee may be Iban or a member of another ethnic group, for the concern in adoption is one of security rather than ethnicity.

A third reason why adoption is frequently practiced is to strengthen ties of friendship and kinship. The gift of a child in adoption to a kinsman or friend is the supreme expression of goodwill.

Finally, adoption may occur between adult peers as, for example, in the case of a sojourner *(orang kampar)* who takes up residence in a longhouse in which he has no kinsmen or friends. When the decision to adopt a sojourner is reached, the intention of the sponsor is made known to other members of the longhouse. The adoption is ritually confirmed before members of the community as the adopting host and the sojourner blend blood *(bekempit ka darah)* from two small wounds which each inflicts upon himself, thereby symbolizing an "openness" of relations which had not existed previously. The two participants are said to have joined mutually in "the adoption of brothers" *(be-ambu' madi')*.

A third way to membership in the *bilik*-family is provided through marriage. Marriages may be arranged in one of six ways. First, a man may enter the family of the woman he wants to marry with no arrangements on the part of his parents. Second, a man may enter the family of the woman through his parents' arrangements. Third, a woman may enter the family of the man if she is received by his parents. Fourth, following the killing of a chicken as an act of expiation, a woman who has delivered a man's child may enter his family if received by his parents. (An unmarried woman who becomes pregnant cannot enter the family of the man until her child has been born.) Fifth, the man is ceremonially taken to the woman's house by members of his family, or if time and resources permit by all the members of his house, and he takes up residence in his wife's *bilik.* Sixth, a ceremony is held involving members of both the man's and woman's kin-groups, and is by far the most elaborate of the forms of marriage.

In each of the six possible ways of marriage, the headman of the community must be informed. In each of the ways attempts are made to obtain the consent of both sets of parents and their siblings who may cause trouble for the couple if they do not approve of the marriage.

The Iban view marriage not as a social affair between the parties involved but in terms of economic implications extending to other persons as well. Prior to marriage, the couple, and in cases of unions approved by the parents and their siblings, their kin-groups discuss with which family the couple will live. This discussion considers the relative advantages and disadvantages of each family if its child moves out to join the other. In the case of a family with many children there is a high probability that some will marry and move out to live with their spouses. On the other hand, a family with only one child may be expected to demand that the child's spouse move in with them. In such a case the parents do not lose a child—they gain a worker.

The rules of residence after marriage are related to the family's control of productive resources. When a person moves out of his family at marriage he loses all rights of inheritance. At the time of separation from his family he is given a portion of the family's common property, including usually one jar and a bronze gong, marking the ties that still exist between the person who is leaving and members of his family who remain

behind. These symbolic gifts are particularly important remind-
ers to his children of relations which may be reactivated. In a
very real sense the person who leaves his family at marriage is
gone but not forgotten.

If the family has an abundance of farmland and gardens, he
may be given a tract of land to prevent his being embarrassed
by in-laws who throw it up to him that he really brought nothing to the marriage. To say that he is given a tract of land means
only that the person is given specific rights to cultivate the land,
for the Iban have not "owned" land in the Western sense of
possessing property; instead families have possessed "rights" to
use the land. Therefore, while a person who leaves his family
loses rights of inheritance—by virtue of his not staying by his
parents until their death—he does retain inalienable rights to
cultivate land, by virtue of the spiritual bond with his ancestors
who cleared the land.

In theory, the person who moves into another family may
return to the annual meeting when sites to be cultivated during
the new horticultural year are discussed and request permission
to farm land to which his natal family holds rights. In practice,
however, when an individual moves into his spouse's family, he
acquires rights to land with other members of his new family
and seldom has occasion to activate the rights to land held by
his natal family.

Members who enter families through marriage often assume
the most important economic roles. Hence, they are granted
rights to land and inheritance in their spouse's family.

Traditional Iban marriage rules are clearly defined. The
forms of marriage which are preferred and those which are
proscribed are commonly recognized. From parents' view,
marriages should be arranged by the parents of the young people involved. Marriage is preferred with a member of one's
kin-group. Marriage should be with a person who stands between the degrees of first and fifth cousin. Marriage should be
monogamous. Marriage, or sexual union, between siblings, parents and children, and grandparents and grandchildren is incestuous. Marriage between a woman and a man who are related
as members of adjacent generations is disapproved, but
propitiatory rites exist to be performed if, for example, an aunt

and nephew—as were involved in one marriage I observed—insist upon marrying.

Iban rules of marriage are rationalized in terms of economic principles. The desire for the marriage of close kinsmen is expressed succinctly in the phrase "(that they may) share fruit, share land" *(saum buah, saum tanah).* One head man explained this phrase in terms of the incest taboo. If siblings marry, he said, their resources would be those of the single family. When cousins marry, on the other hand, the couple shares in land and gardens from both families. Marriage within the kin-group also is said to strengthen kin-ties. Marriage with non-kin is believed to weaken the network of the group by the introduction of strangers to whom some members of the kin-group may have difficulty in relating.

We have considered three ways by which Iban become members of a family: birth, adoption, and marriage. *Incorporation* is a fourth way. When a widowed or divorced woman remarries and takes up residence in her husband's *bilik,* she may bring with her a child by her former marriage. Technically the child has no rights in the new *bilik*-family. Often, however, the child will be granted full membership with the same rights as any other child born to his mother and stepfather.

A second condition under which incorporation occurs is in the case of illegitimacy. If several young men have been entertained by the same woman, who becomes pregnant, all may refuse to admit paternity. In such cases, if the girl does not abort there is no choice for the girl's parents but to incorporate the illegitimate child *(ampang)* into their own family. After appropriate offerings have been made, a pig is slain to expiate any guilt from the family. Thenceforth, the child is said to "claim the pig as father" *(be-apai ka babi)* in lieu of a human father.

Composition of the *Bilik*-Family

The *bilik*-family fluctuates in composition between two and three generations. This fluctuation is due to practices in the care for the young and old, the removal and reentrance of members, and partition.

While theoretically it is possible for more than one child to remain in the *bilik* of birth, I found common residence of parents, married children, and their spouses in only two cases in more than 100 longhouses I visited in the Rejang Valley. The atypical character of these two instances drew the following comment:

Those are most unusual families. Most of us simply could not get along well enough to live together as they do.

Fluctuation within the *bilik*-family is attributable primarily to *bilik* partition. Partition occurs when an individual or family moves out of his natal *bilik* to establish a new and independent unit. Nine of the 37 longhouses in my survey showed an increase in the number of families which could be accounted for solely in terms of partition.

Partition arises primarily from the formation of parallel family units with different and incompatible interests. Within the traditional Iban *bilik,* possessions have been divided into common and private property. Common property has included farmlands, fruit trees, brassware, antique bowls and plates, Chinese jars, ceremonial clothing and ornaments, woven blankets, augury sticks, charms and medicines, sacred and ordinary rice seed, and human skulls.

While the individual Iban might acquire property for himself, he was expected to contribute to the common property of the *bilik* of which he was a member. This was a source of conflict that frequently led to partition. One member might feel that he or his family was contributing more than others. Resentments smoldered and issued forth in gossip, a viable means of releasing hostilities indirectly when other more direct means were proscribed under supernatural sanctions in the community interest. Insults were inferred and added to real injuries, arising from the strain and drain on psychic energies of "always be in sight (of one another)" (*selalu bepeda',* the Iban equivalent of "familiarity breeds contempt"). In the end the individual or family came to the decision that they could tolerate the situation no longer. The decision might be reached in a dream— probably as clear an example of wish fulfillment as could be found—which "compelled" the family or person to move out. The decision might be reached through conversation, in which the parties sought the best solution to their conflict. Occasionally the decision to move out of a family or even from a long-house was reached in the heat of anger, so that the family would leave being scarcely on speaking terms with those who stayed. Gaps in the middle of longhouses mark the removal of their entire section of the house by irate members.

In some cases, children have established separate families because they felt they were being exploited by their parents. I observed a situation of this sort as it developed in the family of Changgan, who has taken the shaman's name Biga', of Rumah Gaong. Changgan is a notoriously casual farmer. In 1970, following the planting of his rice crop, he went on a prolonged shamanic tour of the Oya River communities, leaving his fields untended. His arthritic wife could not walk to the fields, and as a result their total harvest was one large gunny sack of rice. In earlier years Changgan's children did a major part of the farm work, but recognizing their father's indolence and realizing that if they stayed in his family they would never be able to accumulate anything for themselves, they separated from Changgan and built apartments side by side at the end of the longhouse. Despite Changgan's crop failure in 1970—and in subsequent years as well—his children continue to give him rice. Having moved out of the longhouse and built units for themselves, they now are free to work and save for their own personal goals.

Another reason for partition is to act before potential conflict erupts and to make amends for what may have been construed as inappropriate actions. For example, a man in one of the longhouses studied remarried within a year of his first wife's death. Because his wife had been the daughter of a chief, or *Penghulu*, some members of the community were incensed, alleging that the widower had not shown proper respect by remarrying so soon. After the man's son by his first wife married and had children, the man decided that it would be in the interest of the two families—and an improvement of his public image—to construct a unit at the edge of the porch, directly opposite his *bilik*. He took a share of the common property, but turned the remainder over to his son, along with the *bilik*. This action helped remove some of the taint of his earlier indiscretion and earned him the praise of other members of the community.

Partition has been a major factor in the sprawl of Iban long-houses over Sarawak. As genealogical depth and the population grow, some persons see one another and interact more often than do others. Factions form on the bases of kinship, friend-ship, mutual aid, and proximity within the house. Members of one group sometimes feel that they are being slighted or taken advantage of by members of another group, and will decide to move out and to establish a new longhouse. The founding of Rumah Nyelang is a case in point. Members of Nyelang's com-munity were more closely related to Nyelang than they were to Imba. Feeling themselves exploited by the astute Imba and his son, Embuas, Nyelang and his followers moved down the Salim River about twenty minutes' walk from Rumah Imba. (Ironically, Nyelang's followers decided to break away after Imba bought a rice mill and charged his customers for husking their rice. Nyelang promptly bought his own mill which just as promptly broke down, and he and his followers then had to endure not only the ignominy of having their rice milled by Imba but the additional travel as well.)

THE FAMILY IN THE LONGHOUSE

If the *bilik*-family is the fundamental unit of Iban soci-ety, longhouse residence is the most distinctive feature of their organization. Except in a relatively few cases, Iban families belong to longhouses. Even in those situations in which Iban have moved to town, persons often maintain their legal resi-dence in a longhouse.

The longhouse is an attenuated structure comprised of inde-pendently owned family units. A longhouse may include as few as five or as many as seventy such units. The number of units varies in each settlement according to the amount of land avail-able to new members who want to join the community, the relative prosperity of the community, the age and quality of the house, and ties of kinship or friendship between members of the house.

Houses rise on hardwood supports two to fifteen feet above the ground, depending on the lie of the land. In some long-houses the front porch stands ten or more feet high, the back of the house just off the ground; in other houses where the ground falls away toward the rear of the house the front is almost at ground level, the back porch high off the ground.

Family units average about twelve feet in width, so a seventy-family structure is really a *long* house, almost the equivalent of three football fields built end-to-end. When the topography permits, the longhouse is built in a straight line. The former Rumah Nangkai of Pasai was built along the face of a knoll, and had two points at which the units were not parallel to each other but "bent" so that it was impossible to see one end of the longhouse from the other.

Origins of the practice of longhouse domicile are long forgotten. Iban questioned on reasons for the practice attributed it to four principal functions: food-sharing, defense, ceremony, and the administration of customary law. Obviously, these are *post facto* explanations.

Several Iban described longhouse organization as a "unit for survival." They stated that it would be hazardous for a single family to try to live off its own efforts continually, since almost all of them experienced times of food shortages which reduced them to dependence on others.

Every Iban who was asked about the origin of the longhouse related it to a strategy of defense when headhunting was common. Scattered settlements, they said, would have been easy prey to raiders, hence families banded together for mutual defense.

Ceremonial functions realized in the longhouse are considered important ecologically and sociologically. As we shall see, rituals contribute to success in farming by ensuring a more or less simultaneous progress in the various stages. Festive occasions reinforce the solidarity of the community, provide opportunities for the renewal of ties with distant kinsmen and friends, and present a means of upward mobility through demonstration of largesse.

Customary law has been defined and administered in the longhouse context. The longhouse into which an Iban is born, marries, or moves is recognized as his legal residence even though he may work and reside in another area for eleven months out of the year. Through maintenance of his legal residence in a longhouse, a member retains rights to construct a family unit on the community building site *(taba')*, and references to any land to which he has rights by birth. These references are important because, as should be apparent, conflicting claims to the same tract of land often arise because of the flexible and ramifying kinship system. In such cases it is most advantageous to have the support of knowledgeable witnesses of one's longhouse, without which a claimant would be one against many.

Divisions in the Longhouse

The longhouse appears to visitors to be a single structural unit, and tourists—and even longtime, non-Iban residents—speak of "communal living." In fact, the longhouse is an aggregate of independently owned family units. Materials used in the construction of individual units reflect this feature of family independence. In the same house, building materials traditionally have included thatch or ironwood shingles for the roof, bark and rough-hewn planks for walls, and flooring of split bamboo or hardwoods.

The head of the house builds the first section—usually including the family room, verandah, and porch—and other families attach their units on either side, extending the length of the house. Commonly, the families who live closest to the headman's unit include a sibling or cousin, and sections of longhouses represent to varying degrees clustered factions of kinsmen and friends.

Seen from the side, family units are divided by walls from the verandah. Walls also divide each family room *(bilik)* from the next, so that access must be gained through a door leading off the verandah. These walls structurally express the discreteness of each family. In contrast to the longhouse forms of some other Bornean groups, such as the Bisaya, walls between family units do not contain doors to provide access from one apartment to the next. Depending on personal relations, the walls may contain small openings which permit conversation and food sharing between adjoining families. When ill-feelings arise, the windows are boarded over.

It is possible to distinguish four sections in the traditional longhouse, progressing from the front to the rear of the longhouse (see Figure 4). This is the way the visitor enters and proceeds into the house. It also reflects the Iban orientation to

Figure 4. The traditional longhouse.

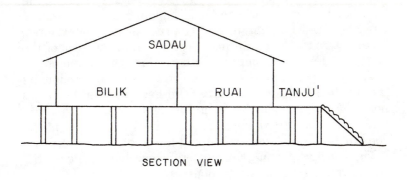

SECTION VIEW

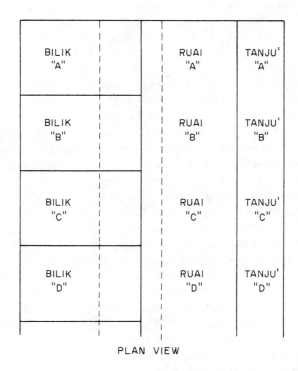

PLAN VIEW

the "high" front where honored guests enter in contrast to the "low" rear where females reside. (The longhouse is sometimes described as an organism; during pregnancies, for example, neither husband nor wife may descend from the rear of the house, for fear the infant will be born through the rectum.)

The open porch *(tanju')* onto which one steps after climbing the notched log varies in width from five to fifteen feet. This porch extends in an unbroken line along the front of the house. Ironwood *(Eusideroxylon zwageri)* is used exclusively in the construction, which must withstand the tropical rains and sun.

The quality of materials and craftsmanship shown in the porch varies from house to house and even from family to family. Differences are immediately evident to the visitor with his first steps onto the porch. Some are a peril to life and limb, being old and apt to collapse, or casually fashioned of loosely laid, roughhewn, irregular slats that shift treacherously underfoot. In other houses the planks are firmly tied with creepers or secured with nails.

The competitiveness which marks much of Iban life is clearly expressed in residents' comments about their unit, house, community, and others. Iban view the longhouse and its units as indicators of the relative wealth of the residents. While he may appear casual about the quality of his house, the Iban is comparison prone and quick to point out the faults in another unit or house which may be in worse repair, older, or dirtier than his own. Similar criticisms are made about other communities.

In addition to providing the first clue to the wealth and conservatism of a community, the porch is the site of various activities. Vines strung between ironwood posts are used for drying clothing. Rice and pepper are spread on mats to dry. At night, men and boys relieve themselves from the outer edge rather than going down to the ground. If healing rites performed in "lower" parts of the house have been ineffective, the shaman will move "up" to the porch, which is the highest place in the house and the terminal point of certain types of ritual. (In the hierarchy of healing rituals, the site of last resort is on the ground directly in front of the house.)

One passes from the porch to the covered verandah or *ruai.* The *ruai* also reveals much about the relative wealth of each family, materials varying from split bamboo to hardwood planks. Reflecting the outgoing orientation and direction of life, flooring pieces extend from the inner to the outer wall. The *ruai* is covered by a roof and extends without division the entire length of the longhouse, allowing traffic to move up and down the house.

The verandah is separated from the family rooms by the "dog's wall" (*dinding udok*). This wall is attached to the main supporting posts of the ridgepole. The dog's wall is the true center of the house—dividing the public and private, male and female domains. Roofs slope down on either side of the ridgepole above it, over the verandah to the front and the family rooms to the back.

The width of the verandah varies from house to house but is fairly even in any single house. In temporary houses which are built after a former residence has been abandoned and before a new house can be occupied, the verandah is narrower than in permanent structures. For example, the verandah in the temporary house of Penghulu Meringgai of Durin was only about eight feet wide; in his new house it is twenty-five feet wide. The verandahs of Rumah Nyala, Nyelang, and Imba range from twenty to twenty-four feet in width, and Rumah Gaong about eighteen feet.

On most verandahs there are three divisions, each marked by supporting posts. Next to the outer wall is an area known as the *padong*, in older houses the place of elevated sleeping platforms (*panggau*). This platform was raised about one foot above the floor level and provided a place for young, unmarried men to sleep. Inside the *padong* is the *ruai* proper, or the area used as the walkway for the house. Each family is responsible for keeping the *ruai* in good repair, and in case of injury resulting from obvious neglect the owners may be made to pay a fine in addition to repairing their section of the *ruai*. The third section is the "place of the rice-mortar" (*tempuan lesong*) where mills, mortars, thatch, and other objects are kept. Here also firewood is stacked against the wall and fighting cocks tethered before the owner's room.

These three divisions are sites of different activities. The *padong* is one of the most important social centers in the longhouse, an area where men and women do light work such as splitting reeds to be used in weaving baskets and mats. In the evening men and women gather in small groups to talk about their farms or anything that comes to mind. Fittingly these conversations are known as *randau ruai, randau* meaning both conversation and a branching creeper. As people gather, hosts offer brass containers with tobacco and paper, or trays containing areca nuts, gambier leaves, and lime, ingredients for a long-lasting, stimulating quid. The *padong* also has been an important center for socialization of the young, where behavioral patterns are reinforced with stories and legends from Iban history.

The *ruai* proper is a center for ritual events. Although most healing rites begin in the *bilik,* many are followed by performances on the *ruai.* The *ruai* is the location of the "altar" in which farming tools and seed are blessed. Rites of marriage and death are performed on the *ruai,* and in the "Festival of Dead Spirits" *(Gawai Antu)* the *ruai* is the path of warriors and bards to the "Opposite State" *(sebayan)* as well as the roadway of the spirits.

The third major section of the longhouse is the *bilik* or family apartment, a rectangular space enclosed by four walls and varying in size and appointments from family to family. The family apartment in older houses is unbroken by walls, cooking being done on a low clay hearth to the rear and the family eating on the floor several feet away. In newer houses the cooking area is separated by a wall from the main section of the apartment.

The size of the *bilik* varies according to the number of family members, relative wealth, and status. In Rumah Gaong the smallest *bilik* was ten feet wide and thirty-two feet from front to back. The largest *bilik* was eighteen feet wide by forty feet deep.

In addition to cooking and eating, the family sleeps and stores its property in the *bilik*. Married men and women sleep in the *bilik,* along with young children. Girls always sleep in either the *bilik* or the loft. From about age ten to twelve, boys sleep on the *ruai* from where they launch their romantic pursuits. All heirlooms and common property are stored in the *bilik,* or if it is too small, in the loft.

The final section in the traditional longhouse is the loft or *sadau* which extends halfway over the verandah. The most common use of the loft is as a storage area, where the large bark-bins containing the family's rice supply are stored. Mats, baskets, and farm tools also are kept in the loft. Some families use the loft as a sleeping area for young unmarried girls or occasional guests. Some rituals take place in the loft. For example, the initiation *(bebangun)* of the shaman moves between main floor and loft—between earth and sky. When owls alight on longhouse roofs, offerings to the spirit represented by the owl are made in the loft just beneath the spot on which the bird was seen. (The owl is a harbinger of death to the Iban, just as he is to some North American Indians, such as the Nootka.)

The Longhouse: A Universe in Microcosm

The longhouse has been the symbolic as well as the actual center of the world for most Iban. Houses have been oriented toward the east in most cases, so that the sun and moon appear to "move" directly over them. Rituals are performed to call heaven and earth to attend to the needs of the residents.

The longhouse is divided into two major sections on both the horizontal and vertical planes. On the first plane, the *ruai* or male sphere is distinguished from the *bilik* or female sphere. On festive occasions men are seated at the highest part of the *ruai*, i.e., along its outer wall, and women enter the *bilik* of relatives and friends. The male's place is on the *ruai*, and the man who spends too much time in the *bilik* is liable to be called "female male" *(laki indu')*. The eastward orientation of the house toward the sun reinforces the maleness of the *ruai* which is entered after a climb upon a notched log which, with its decorated head, is recognized as a phallic symbol.

On the vertical plane, however, it is the female principle that predominates. This structural expression is important to remember, for while Iban men idealize the female who is shy and retiring, who keeps out of sight in the *bilik*, Iban women enjoy a great deal of independence and there are ritual occasions when they "get their own back." For example, during the festival of *Ngelumbong, sebayan* is said to impinge on *dunya* and what normally is prohibited is permitted. Any man who does not want his wife assaulted shuts her in the *bilik*. Women brandish outlandishly large male organs with which they "assault" men.

Rice bins, the "wombs" of Iban subsistence, are kept in the lofts and women have primary access to them. (In the mythical account of the birth of the god Keling's sons, Kumang lays her eggs in a rice bin.) The loft also is the place in which the initiation or transformation of the Iban shaman *(manang)*, whose homosexual tendencies are commonly acknowledged by the Iban, takes place. Subordination of the male principle on the vertical plane is illustrated further by the use of the term *palang (babi)* for both the crosspiece of the house supports and the crosspiece of bone which is inserted into the glans penis, supposedly for the woman's pleasure during intercourse (cf. Harrisson, 1964).

Just as the longhouse is oriented to the sun as the source of life, so the Iban is oriented to his longhouse. Other people live upriver or downriver from the center, which defines his place of belonging and his humanity.

Most Iban continue to look upon the longhouse as the *place* for Iban to live. So strong is the longhouse internalized as the residential norm that Iban who have not lived in a longhouse for years express conflict about their own type of housing, and some actually return to live in the longhouse. For example, according to one Iban who has lived away from the longhouse in Sibu for more than thirty years:

The longhouse is the proper residence. It is there that young people are socialized and develop respect for our ways. Those who have not lived in the longhouse are not really Iban—they are part Malay, part Chinese, part European, and a little Iban. . . . [According to traditional Iban views] the person who lives apart from the longhouse is *Antu Uging*, "evil spirited," for he is a strange person, else why would he want to live alone. He does not share in the life of the longhouse, does not participate in daily activities, and assumes no responsibility for teaching the young.

It is interesting—and important—to note that from the speaker's view, longhouse residence is the crucial feature for Ibanness: "Those who have not lived in the longhouse are not really Iban." They are something else, and they live in another world.

BEYOND THE LONGHOUSE

One of the most common sights in a longhouse is that of a man seated cross-legged on the floor, tying loops into an expanding fishnet. This practice has provided the simile "tying up the fishnet" *(nyambong jala)* to describe how the Iban trace back genealogical ties with strangers. This is among the first ritual acts engaged in by Iban when they enter a strange longhouse. By tracing ties upward through one's parents, grandparents, great-grandparents, and so on, the Iban usually are able to find a common relation, either real or fictional. Thus, an Iban rarely meets a "nonkinsman."

Traveling on the Mukah River with a young Iban man, we entered eighteen different longhouses. He had never been on that river or in the houses where we stayed, so my companion and a member of the host community "tied up the fishnet" or "genealogized" *(betusut)*. With amazing frequency the participants discovered some ancestral tie within five generations, either between themselves or between my friend and an acquaintance of the host.

Iban families are part of a widely ramifying system of kinship that has developed in response to the mobility of Iban settlements. According to needs and opportunities, proximity or distance, groups expand and contract to include and exclude individuals.

Two terms are used by the Iban for groups other than the family unit *(sabilik): suku juru* and *kaban belayan.* The word *suku* means "one-quarter" and *juru,* a word of Sanskrit origin, means "wife." The phrase connotes kin-ties originating with one's grandparents, and includes persons to the degree of first cousin.

The *kaban belayan* is any group of people who share rights of reciprocity with ego. The *kaban* includes kin and also may include non-kin and even non-Iban. In Rumah Nyala, for example, I found that Ganai reckoned Ili and Geranding as members of his *kaban* because they cooperated in various ways, even though neither is Iban by birth. The very vagueness of the concept of the *kaban* and its unclear boundaries are significant aspects of the web of relations which may be drawn tighter or loosened as circumstances prescribe.

The *suku juru* and *kaban belayan* correspond to the kindred. In contrast to lineages which are corporate groups, permanently defined by relations to a founding ancestor, the kindred is a discontinuous group, with no corporate functions, which is activated for occasions such as the birth, marriage, and death of an individual. Despite opinions to the contrary (cf. Freeman, 1961), the Iban include affines or in-laws as well as other kinsmen in statements about the kindred. This we might well expect, given the proclivity of the Iban for adopting persons to "membership" in action groups, of which the kindred is one form. Although the Iban terminologically distinguish "kinsmen" *(kaban mandal)* from "affines" (*kaban tampil,* literally, "joiners"), these distinctions are considered unimportant in actual behavior, which equally includes members of both categories.

Encompassing families and kindred, and extending well beyond them, are sets of ties built upon alliances between members of different communities. Such alliances are of two major types.

The first type is known as "one brotherhood" *(sapengabang),* from "one" *(sa-),* "brother" *(abang),* and the substantive prefix *peng-.* (*Ngabang* means "to visit on ceremonial occasions," or literally "to show oneself a brother.") "One brotherhood" includes members of longhouses which are geographically close to one another. Thus, for example, the people of Rumah Nyala include the communities of Rumah Banta, Emperan Tekalong (across the Igan River from Aup), and formerly the easternmost people of Penasu' in their brotherhood. Through time the number of communities has undergone attrition as, according to the Iban's explanation, "We no longer are as close as we once were."

The brotherhood is a survival of former raiding and headhunting times. Those who fought together against more distant enemies now eat together. It is unthinkable to skip a nearby house in favor of members of a more distant one; hence, every house within an arbitrarily defined region is included in invitations to feasts or other events of moment. Equally, every member of each such house is included automatically.

When major festivals are held, invitations are extended to members of other communities, together with requests for chickens, eggs, and other foodstuffs. Thus the brotherhood also is fittingly known as "food-sharers" *(sapemakai).*

The second type of relationship is based on the felt need and desire expressed to maintain social ties over a greater area. When a festival is being planned, members of the host community indicate which kinsmen and friends beyond the brother-hood they will invite. Persons invited are those with whom close relations have existed in the past, such as kinsmen and friends who have moved to distant houses, or kinsmen in a distant community from which a member of the host group has moved, and with whom individuals want to maintain or renew ties by "checking up on one's share" *(ngabas ungkup)*.

Both types of ceremonial relationships have been important in that they have strengthened good relationships between in-dividuals and communities both near and far through the ex-change of visits, food, labor, and money. "The brotherhood" has promoted a sense of regional solidarity through the activation of localized networks binding nearby communities together as they render aid to one another. By "checking up on our shares" the Iban have maintained an image of continuity which tran-scends the limits of space and time, an image which is actuated periodically through ceremonial exchanges.

THE IBAN

The Iban have lacked any supralocal integration, the most important political group being the longhouse, which joined or ignored regional alliances. The rise of regional chief-doms was precluded by two factors. First, the exchangeable surplus from Iban farms was inadequate to support full-time political leaders. And second, the fierce individualism, seen clearly in the leveling processes of the longhouse in which those who have are pressured into distributing to those who have not, has made the accumulation of material wealth and political capital impossible.

Despite the absence of supralocal integration, and despite their being widely scattered and geographically isolated from one another, Iban communities have maintained a strong sense of unity and ethnic identity. The group of which he is immedi-ately aware is often limited to his longhouse community, cere-monial brotherhood, or region, but the Iban nonetheless readily identifies with fellow Iban of other districts and divisions through the use of a common language, adherence to similar principles of organization, and commitment to a remarkably consistent body of beliefs.

"The ways of grandfathers and grandmothers" *(jalai aki' ini')* have provided a meaningful adaptation to generations of Iban. Resistance to elements of modern culture is often explained precisely in these words—"(the new patterns of behavior, ideas, objects) are not 'the ways of the ancestors' " *(ukai jalai aki' ini' kami Iban)*.

So tenacious are the organizing principles and traditional norms that they continue to endure and serve as boundary markers between Iban and non-Iban in modern contexts. For example, some Iban who have moved from the hills to lowland areas return annually to farm dry rice on ancestral lands. Iban in the town of Sibu have organized *randau ruai*, "discussions on the verandah," so important has been this longhouse institution, even though the Sibu Iban now live in verandahless individual houses.

SUMMARY

Through the development of a common and clearly defined set of organizing principles the Iban established and have maintained their identity and unity. Each Iban has belonged to a *bilik*-family by virtue of birth, adoption, marriage, or incorporation. Most Iban have been members of longhouses, and historically those few families who did not were questionably "Iban."

The longhouse has been the center of Iban life and has symbolized the high esteem which the Iban have held of their ways of life. Longhouse organization probably came into existence because of a variety of reasons—ecological, economic, military—and continues to predominate patterns of residence.

By reference to extensive genealogies and flexible networks the Iban have maintained a strong sense of unity through time and over space. Self-assured by these symbols and confident in the knowledge that they belong and are accepted, the organizing principles of the Iban have provided adaptive advantages in their social evolution.

Chapter 4

IN THE HILLS

The world of the Iban was created in the hills. Iban myths charge the hills as being objects of special creative acts by the gods and as sanctuaries for men in time of trouble. The hills arose as Ara and Irik, creator bird-gods, compressed the earth to fit beneath the inverted wok-like sky. In their editing of the flood myth, the Iban recount how those who fled to the hills lived, while those who remained on the plains perished.

The hills have been the proper zone for Iban because they have been the proper zone for Iban gods (or vice versa). *Panggau Libau,* the home of Keling and other gods (cf. Gerijih, 1964), is a hilly region commanding a view of the earth beneath. The aspiration for ascendancy that marks much of Iban life is symbolized in myths of the omen bird-gods, Sengalang Burong and his seven sons-in-law, whose activities provide prototypical examples for the Iban.

The most powerful spirits live in the hills where the Iban have repaired for vision quests. Upon their return from a profitable trip or a successful raid, the Iban made thank-offerings in the hills *(niat ka bukit).* (As recently as 1971 I observed this rite in a modern form on the occasion of a visit by Linus, a commando, to Rumah Nyala.)

The Iban have been first and foremost hill farmers, rationalizing their selection of the hilly zone in the story of Seragunting, who was half man, half god, and lived halfway between the earth and sky. Choice of the hills probably was due to Iban recognition of the fertility of soils under primary forest. These soils are described in Iban myth as having been created by *Tai' Belut*, "Worm Dirt," an eco-mythical expression which is firmly supported by Scott's soil analyses (1965, 1969) of hilly areas in Sarawak, which revealed numerous worm casts.

Some of the Iban who moved into the Rejang Valley settled in the hills. To this day their descendants defend the superior character of the hills, the residence of "true" Iban. Hill Iban maintain that the hills are "cool" (*chelap*, "healthy") whereas the lowlands are "hot" (*angat*, "unhealthy"), and "high" (*tinggi'*, "dominant") rather than "low" (*baroh*, "inferior").

The hills commonly are spoken of affectionately as places of cleaner water, cooler breezes, higher houses, stronger men, more beautiful women, faster speech, and rice of superior qualities.

HILL RICE FARMING

Although the food quest of the Iban has involved numerous activities, by far the predominant focus of their energies has been the cultivation of hill rice. In the hills a majority of Iban still practice shifting cultivation whose main characteristics are

rotation of fields rather than crops; clearing by means of fire; absence of draft animals and of manuring; use of human labour only; employment of the dibble stick . . . short periods of soil occupancy alternating with long fallow period (Pelzer, 1945: 17).

Rice is not merely a crop or food to the Iban. Rather, hill rice cultivation has been considered by them as the distinctive feature of their culture. In Iban culture it is rice cultivation which separates men from animals. It distinguishes Iban from their remote ancestors "who lived like Punan in the jungle," i.e., gathering and hunting.

In Iban mythology, rice is a gift from the gods. Sengalang Burong, the brahminy kite-god, gave the first seed to Seragunting together with instructions about its cultivation. The divine directives also specifically prescribed the replacement of tubers —on which they previously had subsisted—with rice. (The supplanting of tubers with rice is a common feature in the myths and rituals of the hill tribes of Southeast Asia. This feature probably indicates a transition from vegetative reproduction, i.e., planting cuttings, to seed reproduction, and a widespread preference for rice due in part to its greater storability.)

In a mythological variant, rice is described as a treasure stolen. Two culture heroes observed a goddess—note the female cultivator who possesses the "seed"—growing rice. Rice was unknown to them and they were determined to get some of the seed. Their requests were repeatedly denied. Two attempts to steal some of the rice seed were unsuccessful. On the third try, one of the men placed three seed under his foreskin where the goddess failed to look when she searched him. The two heroes returned to the Iban, planted the seed, and introduced rice farming.

"In the beginning there was rice," a gift from Ini' Rajah Pipit, the grandmother of the Sparrow King, to Dayang Petri, the daughter and seventh child of the gods. Unlike her older siblings who ate charcoal, Dayang Petri refused to eat anything but rice. (Again, note the origin of rice with females.) In the edenic situation, the rice was as large as a mango or grapefruit. Once planted it lived for years. The reaping baskets walked to the farm where the waiting rice jumped into them until they were full and then the baskets walked home. Paradise was lost, alas, when Dayang Petri impatiently slashed some of the rice to reap it herself, and then mischievously startled the baskets. (The Iban generally dislike being startled, suffering the universal psychobiological feeling of shock that is expressed in terms of "soul loss." By analogy they extend this dislike to plants, animals, and even inanimate objects.) The marvelous properties of the rice and baskets were lost, and from that time on the Iban were reduced to producing rice by the sweat of their brow and by carrying the baskets which previously had carried their food for them.

As with other hill tribes in Southeast Asia, rice cultivation is not merely a technique for acquiring food but a total way of life that is supported by and in turn reinforces Iban theology, cosmology, and eschatology.

The basic premise upon which rituals observed in connection with rice cultivation are founded is that rice, as well as all other objects, has a soul *(samengat)*. Rice, however, in contrast to other objects, is peculiarly related to the Iban for it is enlivened by the soul of the ancestors. Rice nourishes man who dies to give essence to rice, and so the circle of life continues. The strong orientation of many features of Iban life to rice cultivation and its various rituals warrant our describing traditional Iban adaptation as a padi-culture.

To eat implicitly means to consume rice. The first food the infant tastes after his mother's milk is rice gruel. In adult life there is no more certain measure of individual ability and family worth than success in rice farming.

We once entertained some Iban guests for a meal of roast beef, potatoes, beans, and congealed salad. We purposefully served Western fare, having been made sensitive to the fact that Iban rarely had an occasion to eat such food, for when they were entertained in the homes of Westerners their hosts tried to provide food familiar to the Iban. After our guests left, my wife and I had to go to the market. To our consternation, we saw in a nearby coffee shop our Iban guests wolfing down plates of steamed rice. "Didn't you have enough to eat in our house?" we asked with genuine concern. "Oh yes," was the reply of one of the men, "but we really hadn't eaten—there was no rice!"

Extrapolating from their horticulture—and possibly reflecting early Indian influences—the Iban have developed a cyclical concept of existence that I have mentioned before but now want to fill out. At death, the soul of the Iban is ritually separated and apprised of the fact that it is dead. The dead soul is compared to a withered flower which must be severed from the stalk lest it infect other members of the family.

The soul crosses "the bridge whose crossing makes anxious" *(Batang Titi Rawan,* an apt expression for death) and enters "the opposite state" *(sebayan),* discussed earlier. After a period of self-indulgence, gluttony, drinking, and reveling with members of the opposite sex, the soul then proceeds on a journey through a series of river valleys. The journey is a complex one, and as recounted on the memory boards used by Iban chanters, retraces the wanderings of the Iban. Although each name is significant in the mytho-history of the Iban, the most important valleys are "Suffering" *(Mandai Awai),* "Death" *(Mandai Mati),* and "Peace" *(Mandai Jenoh).* At the last stage the soul is changed into rice-nourishing dew to descend upon and enliven the grain, thereby ensuring "soul" in the rice. ("Soul-food" would be a readily comprehensible concept to the Iban.)

The ritualization of Iban horticulture prevents our distinguishing between natural and supernatural spheres, if, indeed, such a distinction is ever possible in the Iban world. In aboriginal culture, techniques and rituals undoubtedly developed concurrently as ways of ensuring success in farming and achieving a modicum of unity, particularly at critical stages in the farming year. It seems appropriate, therefore, to consider ritual and technology together, for while a topical dissection is possible and might be useful for analytical purposes, to the Iban they are parts of a single living body of culture.

THE FARMING YEAR

The beginning of the farming year is marked by an annual meeting called by the head of the house. This meeting is held at the end of April, after the previous year's crop has been brought to the house and stored. This meeting is extremely important, being designed to achieve some approximation of simultaneity in each family's progress. The meeting also serves to remind members of the community that they are an ecological unit in which group survival is more important than individual success.

The head of each family in the house attends for the purpose of discussing the family plots to be farmed during the new year. This permits the families to state where each will farm and to avoid potential conflicts due to overlapping claims to the same ancestral lands. Members who have moved away may attend the meeting to activate their rights to cultivate land held by their natal families. Although this seldom happens, Roth's reference (1896: 419) indicates that the practice is of some antiquity.

Renting land is not common, given the relative abundance available to most families. When requests to rent a farm site are made—due primarily to the alleged fertility or proximity of the farm—they are presented at the meeting, and if an agreement is reached then payment at the rate of one-half bushel of rice per acre is accepted by owner and renter.

The farming year is marked in its stages by a host of rituals.

These rituals are emphasized to greater or lesser degrees in all communities, and differences in the names of the rituals indicate localized emendations. Counting all minor acts, farm rituals exceed four dozen. Generally, however, about one dozen rites are observed to mark the progress of farmers and farms from one stage to the next. These rituals include the following major liturgies from the beginning to the end of the farming year.

1. The Festival of the Whetstones *(Gawai Batu)*
2. The First Augury *(Beburong)*
3. Confirming the Site *(Manggul)*
4. Visiting the Burned Site *(Ngabas Tegalan)*
5. Planting Sacred Rice *(Nanam Padi Pun)*
6. Tabooing the Fields *(Ngemali Umai)*
7. Washing Off the Charcoal *(Masu' Arang)*
8. Breaking (New) Rice *(Matah Padi)*
9. Carrying Harvest Mats *(Nganjong Penyedai)*
10. Harvesting *(Negetau)*
11. Storing *(Besimpan)*
12. Discarding the Pollen *(Muai Miang)*

Mention will be made of the rituals in the sequence they are observed, but it is impossible to discuss each in detail. We shall consider the Festival of the Whetstones because of its importance and because it has many features that are common to other Iban rites.

Gawai Batu

The date for the first major farm ritual, the Festival of the Whetstones, is set at the annual meeting. At that time each family indicates which guests it will invite.

The days prior to the festival are frenetic with preparations. Rice beer is prepared, men hunt and fish, vegetables are collected, and the guests invited. Invitations to "food-sharers" are accompanied by requests for eggs and chickens, which will be repaid when guests turn hosts. Bonds are forged through balanced reciprocity, and exchange is a principal facet of Iban ritual activities. Guests must be invited, not only in the interest of network maintenance but also because they personify the mythical visit of Pulang Gana, the god of fertility, and his family, whose visit to the house and farms is anticipated as the focal point of the festival.

On the day of the festival, guests who come from other houses bathe and dress before being received at the foot of the ladder by male hosts. The guests are led up the notched ladder at the south end of the longhouse and onto the covered verandah. There they are received before each family's apartment with liquid refreshments: rice beer and home-distilled whiskey, formerly, and now in addition, commercial whiskey, brandy, and beer. Male guests traverse the "universe," moving along the verandah from south to north. When they reach the northern end of the verandah, they are led back along the outer edge or the preeminently male section of the house just inside the front wall. "To the top, to the top, friend" *(Katas, katas, uai)* is urged upon each guest, the outgoing orientation of the Iban being structurally expressed in the designation of the outer wall as "the highest place." As the women and girls move past the receiving line and come to the apartments of close kin or friends, they drop out of the line and enter the apartments, the "female" or back section of the house.

Iban rituals involve the repetition of clearly defined acts in numbers of three to seven, a fact that will be noted in connection with various farming activities. It is well to remember that the Latin *ritus,* from which "ritual" is derived, means "number." We have mentioned the three grains of rice stolen from the gods. Fittingly, the harvest begins with the cutting of three panicles. Dayang Petri was the seventh child, and seven items is an optimum for offering baskets.

After the men have been seated, three acts are performed to ensure the success of the festival and the fortune of the new farming year. First, guests are told that if they have observed any omen bird, snake, or any other unfavorable sign on their way they are to disregard it; an offering will be made to appease the spirit represented. Second, one of the hosts, grasping a chicken by legs and breast, waves it over the heads of the guests at the same time pronouncing a blessing upon them. After the chicken has been killed, each person's forehead is touched with a feather dipped in the chicken's blood to symbolize protection, community, and a vicarious participation in death to the old year if the previous harvest has been poor. Third, the head men from other houses—in teams of three each—admonish the men seated on each verandah to put away hard feelings, for no quarreling or fighting will be tolerated during the festival. (The word "admonish" also means "bezoar stone" *(geliga)*, and an acceptance of the admonition—just as a bezoar stone—is an aid to success.

Following a communal meal, an elderly guest who is noted for his personal success and who is free from adultery makes an offering to the gods of fertility. The man chosen must be successful, and it is hoped that some of his good fortune will extend to his hosts. He must be free from adultery for human sexual behavior is analogous with and important to the development of the rice crop. As with man, so with rice, and vice versa. Because of the socially unacceptable pregnancies—though not the sexual acts *per se*—by which bastards are conceived, such persons are prohibited from entering the rice fields of other families, lest the rice die.

To make the offering the man moves onto the uncovered front porch and sits on three woven grass mats placed one above the other. Finely designed blankets are hung above and around him, focusing the attention of the world and its forces on his acts. A whetstone from each family is placed in a wooden trough in front of him. A pig is placed squealing over the trough, and combed with water, its hindlegs and forelegs securely tied. When the pig is calmed—again note the avoidance of shock—the man swiftly pierces its heart with a spear and the blood runs into the trough and over the whetstones. The sacrificial act is followed as the man takes from various containers areca nuts, gambier leaves, glutinous rice, eggs, various rice cakes, and pieces of fish, blending them together in an offering connoting subsistence and surplus.

The offering is placed into the trough with the stones and the man invokes the god and goddess of fertility, Pulang Gana and Anda Mara, to help their devotees, to protect them, and to give them rice. A portion of the prayer to Pulang Gana and Anda Mara expresses the purpose of the acts.

Gods of our grandparents, Gods of our parents, visit altogether, advance as one. . . . Let the gods from the earth arise, from the rich soil let them lift up their waists. . . . Bring cakes, medicines, magical stones, and boars' tusks to shape the land and make it fertile.

Bring the stone of inexhaustibility to use in storage, to change scarcity into surplus.

Bring the rice stone that our rice may increase with the swelling of the tides. May we farm without weariness, clearing the undergrowth and finding magical rice. May we cut the heads with no feeling of fatigue, having strength to fish and strike the heads of the rice-fish.

After the invocation, the pig's liver is cut out and the ventricles examined to divine the success of the coming farm work. Failure to obtain a propitious reading may result in the sacrifice of a second pig.

The whetstones are removed and each family places its stone in a ritual center on its covered verandah. The movement of activities from the central site on the porch, where all of the whetstones are collected, to the verandah where each stone is placed separately on its family's section is instructive, indicating the flow of Iban energies and attention between unity and diversity.

Stone, weeding knives, bushknives, hoes, sickles, and axes, together with baskets of seed are covered with a woven blanket to form each family's ritual center. Within the blanket is also hung a ceremonial basket, with a part of a lily, a piece of bamboo, and porcupine quills. The lily *(senkenyang)* is of a species planted close to growing rice to protect it. The bamboo represents a small trap in which it is hoped a blessing from Pulang Gana will be captured. The porcupine quills symbolize the creator of the earth, Raja Samerugah, father-in-law of Pulang Gana, who will help to command the presence of the god of fertility.

At dusk, bards begin to intone the invitations asking Pulang Gana and his company to come. Other gods such as Keling and his consort, Kumang, come, but Pulang Gana delays. (Note the absolute cruciality attached to Pulang Gana's appearance; even Keling, probably the most popular of the gods, cannot stand in his stead.)

Keling and Kumang suggest that messengers be sent, whereupon *Nendak*, the white-rumped Shama and son-in-law of Sengalang Burong, carries the invitation to the house of the Wind Spirit. The Wind Spirit quickly whisks away to the house of Pulang Gana relaying the invitation to him. Pulang Gana starts for the feast with his wife, daughter, son-in-law, and two slaves. His progress is reported in the chants of the bards.

Between four and five o'clock in the morning the company arrives at the house. The gongs are struck immediately and a procession is formed to give the party an honorable reception. The procession moves around the verandah seven times. An offering is made of a white fowl after the party has divided into two lines: the men with whom Pulang Gana and his son-in-law are seated, and the women with whom his wife and daughter sit. Pulang Gana and his son-in-law give the men charms to grow rice, his wife and daughter give gifts to the women to help them weave and to attend to domestic tasks.

The names of the gods are aggregates of Iban values. Pulang Gana's wife is "Fertile Land Who Caps the Bamboo," and his daughter is "Seed Dissolving in the Soil, Maid of the Pleiades until Ready." His son-in-law's name combines courage and status," "*Haji* (One Who Has Made the Pilgrimage to Mecca) Brave to go beyond the Moon seeking wealth." Pulang Gana's slaves are the loris, "The Bachelor Who Distributes," and the tarsier, "Father of the Generation of Those Who Strike."

Augury

Taking auguries is part of the Festival of the Whetstones in some houses, a separate ritual in others. In either case, the various forms augury takes are crucial to the prognosis for farming and a sense of confidence. In most houses another meal is eaten to celebrate the arrival of Pulang Gana and members then prepare to take auguries. Only after he has arrived can the Iban look to higher things.

Iban augury involves the observation and marking of bird flights and calls. At the beginning of the agricultural year, three bird sticks are broken off after *Nendak* has been seen flying from the left, then two more when he is seen flying from the right, and finally one for *Embuas (Rufous piculet)*, another son-in-law of Sengalang Burong.

The families then go to their respective fields where they hold the sticks and ritually "sweep" the sites with them. Taking a clump of earth, the family head prays that it may be fertile.

Three sticks are selected as a foundation for the whetstone. An offering, prepared earlier in the longhouse, is buried to ensure the soil's fertility. The earth is struck three times with a bushknife which then is resharpened on the whetstone. This is repeated twice, after which the parties return to the longhouse, leaving the stones at the farm sites. The farms are under taboo and cannot be visited for the next three days.

Confirming the Site

Near the end of May or the first of June, the farm site is ritually confirmed. This rite, *Manggul,* is observed according to the appearance of the Pleiades on the horizon at dawn. The importance attached to the ritual confirmation varies according to each community's tradition. In some it is observed as a part of the whetstone festival; in others, as a separate rite. In any event, the order is similar and the requests expressed in the prayers are essentially the same as those made in the first festival. For example, the prayer delivered at the site being confirmed asks that

if the land is worn and used, acrid and foulsmelling, reeking of urine and offal, may it be changed to become land that is arable and light, land that is fat and rich, land that can become, that is clean, land that will bring us good fortune. May all planted on this land be luxuriant, multiplying, increasing, bearing, that our rice may hang heavy and full-headed.

Beyond the obvious social function of renewing ties between participants, and the psychological function of allaying anxieties and giving confidence, these festivals have a further heuristic value in concentrating individual and community efforts in a simultaneous start in the horticultural year. Ritual regulations serve to ensure a synchronization of activities, the importance of which becomes most apparent in the later stages of the rice growth when fields are besieged by sparrows. The first month could well be called "the month of prayer for Iban unity." It is one feature of the Iban's plan for survival, for the farmer who is either too early or too late will almost certainly have his crop reduced more severely by birds than the farmer whose fields progress with his fellows'. In the words of one notoriously successful farmer, "If we are to get rice, we cannot be much ahead or much behind others. Otherwise, we plant for the birds." Hopefully, if rice progresses at about the same rate, the birds will spread themselves over more farms and the loss in any single field is less.

Clearing

By mid-June the work of clearing the farm sites begins. The initiation of this work is marked with an offering to protect the workers from injury and to forestall any bad omen that might require the family to call off its work and move to another site. Offerings are made in every event of moment so that, as expressed in the words of one Iban leader, "Nothing is undertaken without the appropriate offerings."

On the first day, small saplings are cut in an area not exceeding two square poles. The purpose is to apprise the land gradually of the intention of the farmers, for neither Iban nor land like to be startled. On succeeding days, longer periods are given to clearing, and progressively larger plants and greater areas are cut. In upland areas this stage is marked by the use of the bushknife.

The clearing of recent secondary growth on land that has lain fallow for up to seven years is an extension of this stage. Such sites may be cleared entirely with the bushknife. The clearing of older secondary growth is different, and on sites uncultivated for fifteen years or more trees may measure up to three feet in girth. Clearing of older growth commonly requires the use of either the traditional axe-adze *(beliong)* or the European axe *(kapak)*. Women and boys help in clearing the smaller plants and trees, but the cutting of the larger trees is men's work.

Felling

After the undergrowth has been cleared, the trees are felled. In virgin forest where little light penetrates, there is little undergrowth in the shade of the giant trees which may stand 150 to 200 feet tall. The felling of these trees on steep hillsides separates the men from the boys. The task requires nerve, foresight, physical strength, and agility, and is a formidable task even to skilled Iban men. Consequently there are some men much more able to undertake the dangers of felling the large trees than are other men.

Felling usually proceeds from smaller to larger trees. Commonly, trees will be cut in rows to fall away from the next line to be cut. This permits removal of the branches of the trees that are cut, and their piling for drying. Progressing in this way, men are unencumbered as they move on up the hill to the next line.

Drying

There is no more crucial period to the success of shifting cultivation than the time just after the clearing of the farm site. In addition to consideration of astrological phenomena, such as the positions of the Pleiades, Orion, and Sirius, the Iban have planned their farming schedule to take advantage of the short dry season between the end of the southwest monsoon in late July and the onset of the northeast monsoon in late September or early October. Ideally, a dry period of from one to four weeks will develop, sufficient to dry the undergrowth and branches that have been cut, and to achieve a complete burning of the debris.

"We must await the dry season and never expect the dry season to await us," stated one Iban. Yet the occurrence of the dry season earlier than expected *may* find it waiting for the farmers, and an accurate prediction of weather conditions is almost impossible. A short dry spell may occur in May or September, or any time between those months. It may last four days, after which heavy rains set in and soak the cuttings. It may last four weeks, extending into the planting season so that seed will not sprout. It may develop in one valley and not the next.

The chancy character of the rainfall is influential in the reluctance of Iban farmers to invest energy and time in the onerous and often useless task of lopping branches and piling them for more thorough burns. While many Iban recognize the advantages of such work, few are willing to perform it. The uncertainties of the rainfall are too great. If a long dry season develops, the cuttings will burn anyway. If it does not develop, then the work is for nothing. From the view of the Iban farmer, the success of the burn really is a matter of fortune.

Burning

Farms are fired usually in the months of August and September, although occasionally enterprising farmers who are ready take advantage of short dry seasons in late July. Some farmers are forced to wait for later dry spells. For example, in

1970 some Iban of the Mujong, a tributary of the Balleh, did not burn their farms until early October.

When a large number of farms are fired for several days in succession, a blanket of smoke and fine debris lies heavily over the valleys. Thus the intense heat which accompanies the dry season becomes even more oppressive.

Farms are burned with attention being given to natural and social boundaries. To prevent the spread of flames to nearby trees, firebreaks are made by preliminary burning of a strip around the perimeter of the farm. When farms adjoin the lands of other farmers, customary Iban law requires that the families confer to avoid personal accidents or even death, and to avoid any possible damage to the whetstone of another family, the stone having been left at the farm after the earlier festivals.

Ideally, farms are fired at the foot of the slope and from the several touches of the bark-torches, the flames catch the up-drafts and race up the slope. Even on tableland I have observed the rapid progress of flames across the farms, consuming the cuttings and leaving only charred stumps. Often, however, the fires have to be set several times, beginning at the foot of the farm and proceeding upward. When the burning of a field is incomplete, the remaining material must be gathered and piled along the edges, accumulated in piles here and there about the farm, or if the farm is cut by a gully the remaining debris may be thrown into it.

The clearing of a hill-farm is at best incomplete. Planting goes on around the stumps, unconsumed trunks of trees, and amidst piles of unburned branches. In part the incompleteness of the clearing is purposeful. The Iban are quick to point out that a thorough removal of the vegetation, especially on steep slopes, only accelerates the rate of erosion. But recognition of this fact often is transformed into a nifty bit of rationalization for a very inadequate clearing of the farmland.

A complete burn has several advantages. First, it lightens the job of clearing debris. Second, it destroys many of the noxious weeds that compete with the rice. Third, it drives away the hosts of insects that thrive in the plant shade. And finally, it provides potash to the soil. Unlike the practices of some African and other Southeast Asian societies, the Iban neither spread the branches before the burn nor do they spread the ash after-wards.

Planting

Hill-farms are planted by men and women, between whom there exists a clear division of labor. Men dibble, women sow. The dibble stick used by the men is made of hardwood and pointed at the lower end. A circular cross section between three to six inches from the lower end regulates the depth of each hole that is punched in the soil. Iban men use both hands in dibbling, punching holes that are about three inches deep and an inch and a half in diameter.

Women develop a high proficiency for sowing rice seed. By middle age most women are able to flick the seed into the holes from a distance of fifteen inches. Most women carry or have tied at their waists a small basket of seed that is replenished from a larger basket at the foot of the slope. On an average, women place ten seed to each hole, or slightly twice more than the number indicated in the Iban couplet on sowing which says that they plant

One for the rat, one for the sparrow,
One for the pig, and one for us.

The size of the farm depends upon the size of the labor force available and the requirements of the family. In aboriginal times the amount of land that could be cleared by men and cultivated by women was undoubtedly a major factor in determining the horticultural pattern. Few farms are less than one-half acre or more than four acres, and most average about two and one-half acres.

During the agricultural year, labor-exchange groups are formed to share in the tasks of sowing, weeding, and reaping. The pleasant aspects of having friends to work and talk with makes labor exchange the rule for most women, who initiate and arrange such exchanges. "If there is someone else to talk with, the work doesn't seem long and there is no feeling of fatigue," said one woman. Labor exchange is based upon strict rules of reciprocity, with a close accounting of days spent on another's farm and the time owed to one's farm. In most, although not all cases, groups are formed by friends who work together in all of the more labor-demanding tasks. In a few instances, women may participate in different labor groups at different times of the year.

Planting Patterns

Hill-farms are planted with attention to the maturation rates and relative sizes of the grain. The planting of a farm requires a familiarity with the rate at which the rice will ripen so that harvesting can progress from one variety of rice to another without having to skip an unripened strain. To have to do so is impractical as well as theologically unthinkable, for it would create a barrier in the paths of the souls of the rice already harvested.

"Job's tears" and other quick-ripening rices are the first planted. The factor of photoperiodism is important in the maturation of "Job's tears," which is imperfectly filled out if planted too late in the year. The quick-ripening varieties are planted because of seasonal shortages that occur before a new harvest, and because of a keen desire of the Iban to eat new rice as soon as possible.

The size of the rice grains has figured in the planting schemes of the Iban who contend that the souls of the small-grained rice do not mix well with the souls of the large-grained varieties. Iban ethnoscience has developed a firm appreciation for the biological fact that variety is the essence of life, and as a result the Iban historically have perpetuated dozens of strains of rice. Once a subspecies has developed, it is incumbent on the Iban to retain some of the seed for the future. The ecological soundness of this botanical practice is evident.

Over years each family has been able to build up a variety of strains. Stories about prolific bearing rice spread rapidly, and the mobility of the Iban who are eager to acquire new species has helped to disseminate the varieties over great distances. Each variety is given a name, reminiscent of its place of origin (for example, *Lassa, Limbang*), its bouquet *(Uangi)*, or its property *(Pulut)*. These rices are known as the annual rices *(padi taun)* and provide the principal staple of the Iban diet.

The last rice to be sown in hill-farms is the "rice of origin" *(padi pun)*, a special strain of rice arbitrarily but carefully chosen by each family for its distinctive characteristics. It is a cardinal mark of family unity and continuity. Theoretically any of the several dozen varieties of rice commonly cultivated may be chosen as a family's *padi pun*, but once chosen the rice becomes the life-symbol of the family. The sowing of the sacred rice designates the ritual center of the farm. Nearby is planted the lily *(senkenyang),* noted in the Festival of the Whetstones, to guard the growing rice. The *padi pun,* supported by the "rice of attachment" *(padi sangking),* sacred but less important rices, are the last to be harvested and are ritually cut on the final day of harvest. The *padi pun* is never sold or given away, except to members who leave the family to begin units of their own.

Catchcrops are also planted in the farms. Maize is sown in spaces between the different varieties of rice. Cucumbers, pumpkins, eggplants, mustard greens, and longbeans are grown amidst the rice.

Weeding

The onerous and irksome task of weeding actually commences before the sowing is completed, for weeds begin to appear within three or four weeks of the burn. Weed growth varies considerably with the type of land that is being farmed. On plots of newly cleared primary forest the growth is much less than on sites of recent secondary growth. Successive farming of the latter type sites leads to a takeover by weeds, particularly sedges such as *lalang (Imperata cylindrica)* and such shrubs as *resam* and *kemunting.*

In a majority of cases weeding is done superficially, once over by women assisted in a small number of cases by older men. Aversion to weeding seems to be an important contributing factor in the seasonal travels of men. At the completion of planting many men take off and return in time to help with the harvest.

Weeding thus is done principally by women who use a crescent-shaped blade *(ilok),* six inches long by one and one-half inches wide, set in a wooden handle four to six inches long. Occasionally a bushknife is used. The weeds are grasped in the left hand, or pulled toward the worker with an L-shaped branch, then cut as close to ground level as possible.

The casual attitude or downright disdain toward weeding is reflected in the disparate yields received by farmers. Successful farmers account for the failure of other families in terms of the neglect of the latter in keeping their rice fields clear of weeds. In the words of Imba, an invariably successful farmer:

Other people in my house farm this place one year, that place the next, to "see how it feels to move about." They fish, hunt, and neglect their farms, so they don't get enough rice. My farm is so clean that there is no grass, no piece of wood larger than my wrist. It all works out very well for me because even though I don't hunt or fish, I get first choice of any game or fish they take. When I harvest, they are in debt to me for rice that they have borrowed so they even carry my rice into the longhouse.

We may note here that the disparities in yields, reflecting differences in attitudes, planning, and discipline, have likely been a major factor in the persistence of the longhouse as an organizational type. Those who receive surpluses are expected to and expect to share with their less fortunate neighbors.

Tabooing the Field

The absence of effective controls over insects, animals, and birds, and belief in innumerable forces of potential danger to man and rice, have led to a ritual tabooing of the fields *(Ngemali Umai)* upon completion of the first weeding. Offerings are made at the farm with supplications to the spirits of the rat and sparrow *(antu chit, antu pipit)* to eat the rice, cakes, and eggs and then to leave for the sea. When rats are especially numerous an image of a crocodile is molded from clay and appeals are made for the spirit of the crocodile to devour the rats.

After the fields have been tabooed, no one from the family may go to the farm for three days. The paths to the farm are marked with a leaf in the split of a pole that is driven into the ground beside the paths leading to the field. This is a sign to passersby that the field is under taboo, and anyone trespassing on the farm will be subject to a fine.

Guarding the Fields

Except in the case of farms located near longhouses, every family has a farmhouse where members can stay to guard the rice when it heads out. In some cases the farmhouses are individual dwellings. These houses are usually impermanent structures built of split bamboo flooring on bamboo or hardwood supports, with roof and walls of bark, or palm or grass thatch. There are no divisions in the farmhouses, which measure about twelve feet square. The single door opens directly onto an uncovered porch which commands a view of the rice field.

In other cases several families build attenuated farmhouses, similar in plan to the longhouse though smaller and again generally of less durable materials. Such farmhouses are built when families farm adjoining sites. The residents include cognate kinsmen, whose significance we shall discuss later, or families of close friends who often arrange the exchange of labor.

Wild pigs and deer pose a real though often exaggerated threat to rice crops. On occasions such animals do small damage to the new rice and provide a welcomed opportunity to mount a hunt and an outing for men and boys. In areas where forests have been severely reduced, there has resulted a decimation of the animal population and a reduction of losses attributable to pigs and deer.

More serious threats to the rice crops are posed by insects, particularly leaf and plant hoppers *(bengas)*, the Black Shield bug *(empangau rungkup)*, leaf folders *(ulat giling)*, and stem borer *(pasak)*. Other insects that pose much less danger to rice are grasshoppers, locusts, and crickets, all of which are often gathered by small children who roast them over open fires.

Birds and rats are the other major threats to rice, and the damage they wreak emphasizes the importance of an isochronic development of crops. Unless the fields come to fruit at about the same time, the predators will concentrate on those crops that head out earlier or later than the majority over which they spread themselves more sparsely.

Numerous devices are employed to protect the rice against rats and birds. Men build traps, such as the *tinja'* and *panjok*, types of spring-traps with a tread-board and key stick. Young children smear birdlime on sticks which are secured to pegs driven into the ground or to shrubs to catch birds which alight on the gummy birdlime and then cannot free themselves.

As the rice bursts into fruit, sparrows and rats are attracted to the milky, immature grain, and every effort is made to drive them away. The most common attempts consist of hanging lengths of bamboo with hardwood clappers, all with heavy vines leading to the open porch of the farmhouse so that the guards can set the clappers striking to frighten the pests away.

Despite the rituals and techniques aimed at guarding the

fields, some of each year's crop is inevitably lost to insects, animals, and birds. Stories of losses, however, are usually greatly exaggerated. The reasons for exaggeration of losses are several. It permits inefficient or inept farmers to save face. It prevents disappointment if the harvest does not come up to expectations. It protects the remainder of the crop from reprisals by offended spirits and from compliments from a person with the ability to curse crops. (Such a person is believed to cause rice to die on the stalk by simply commenting, "Oh, you have a good crop this year.")

Harvesting

As the rice comes to maturity, an air of excitement marks the behavior of the whole community. This is even more obvious if the previous year's harvest was poor and the people have been eating substitute foods, such as palm cabbages, or, where available, sago starch. Yet even those families with surpluses of rice look forward to tasting the new rice which has a bouquet like that of freshly popped corn.

Harvesting begins with the ritual "breaking of the rice" *(Matah Padi),* lest the soul of the rice be startled. On the morning when the ritual is to be performed, a woman ties together a minimum of three and a maximum of seven panicles with a red thread. After asking the rice soul not to take offense and a prayer that the harvest not be wasteful, the panicles are cut with a harvesting knife. The family and friends then return to the house for rice cakes, beer, and other refreshments.

Harvesting begins in earnest the day after the ritual, with men as well as women helping in the work. Harvesting has its ritual as well as its technical aspects and focuses on the dominant concern with fertility. The lead is taken by the senior active woman who sets the pace in cutting the grain in each family's field. It is she who "fecundizes" or "feminizes"—the Iban term for her pacesetting, *ngindu',* being a verb form of the root *indu'* meaning "woman" or "source." Beginning at the edge of the field, one man or woman reaps straight along the border following the pace of the senior woman who reaps a strip parallel to the first. The reapers move across the first rows, then back to the same side of the field where they began and across again, and so on until a particular variety of rice is finished. If it is necessary for them to cross a path or some natural break in the field, such as a stream, a small stick is laid across the break so that the rice souls may follow the reapers.

On the final day of the harvest a small section of the field wherein stands the sacred rice is reserved for cutting the next morning. The last morning's cutting is a ritualized affair in which the family workers take an offering to the final stand of rice and after a prayer for the sacred rice soul to go with them, the last panicles are cut and carefully placed in a harvest basket that is covered with pieces of the family's clothing, so that the rice soul may be acquainted with the smell of the family. This ritual, *Ngelechut ka Padi*, is performed to ensure that the soul of the rice will move to the longhouse and not stay behind in the ground.

The newly harvested rice is stored temporarily in the farm-house, or if the longhouse is close by it is carried immediately to the longhouse. The carrying baskets, like the smaller baskets used for collecting the panicles when harvested, are made of cane. Carrying baskets stand about three and one-half feet tall and when loaded with rice may weigh as much as 200 pounds. Transporting these baskets up to a mile or more over hill and over streams, sometimes swollen by heavy rains, is no small task, and usually is undertaken by men, although women not uncommonly help in the movement of the rice. My appreciation of the physical strength and stamina of the relatively smallish Iban increased considerably when I had the first carrying basket loaded with rice placed on my back. With knees threatening to buckle and back muscles crying out in protest, I carried the basket only with the greatest effort. It is understandable that whenever possible the Iban load the baskets into boats and take them as near as possible to the longhouse. In some cases, however, movement by water is impossible and the arduous task of overland transportation is necessary.

Threshing and Drying

After the rice has been received ceremonially into the house, preparations are made for threshing. Should any rice be spilled in its transporting, a "spirit-ladder" in the form of a sapling is extended from the family room to the ground so that the soul may come up.

On the day that threshing begins the family serves rice cakes, beer, and whatever other food and drink they may be able to furnish. All members of the community are invited and a sense of festivity fills the house.

The rice is emptied from the carrying baskets into a heap on the covered verandah of the family doing the threshing. A bushel at a time is taken from the pile and placed onto a special mat known as *tikai senggang*. This mat is made of large cane fibers and is not used for any other activity. To sit on it is unthinkable, for it would offend the rice soul. When I asked a several Iban on different occasions whether the *tikai senggang* could be used in any other way, they looked at me incredulously as if I were insane and replied emphatically that of course it could not—didn't everyone know that *tikai senggang* could be used only for the threshing and storing of rice!

Threshing usually is done by men, although in the absence of male workers women will do it. If labor exchange has been arranged for other activities, it is likely for members of the group to share in threshing. Threshers grasp a bark-cloth strap tied securely to an attic joist to balance themselves as they tread the panicles. The threshers separate the grains from the panicles, treading on them with bare feet and swirling the panicles back onto the heap for more treading.

After the first threshing in which many grains are loosened, women squatting at the sides of the mat lift the panicles and sift any free grains through their fingers onto the mat. The panicles then are gathered up again for a second threshing by foot.

As the rice is threshed it is spread onto a large mat *(bidai)* used especially for drying the rice on the family's uncovered porch. The rice is poured onto the mat and raked with a long-handled wooden blade to a depth of about one inch. Lengths of bamboo or thin wooden poles twelve feet long or longer are extended from windows opening from the verandah onto the porch so that hungry chickens can be driven from the drying rice with a swing of the pole. Ideally, the rice will be dried for a full day to assure that it will not mold in storage. The first drops of a shower, therefore, send men and women alike scurrying to cover the rice or to bring it into the house in case of a hard rain.

After the rice has been dried, it is returned to the covered verandah and covered by folding the corners of the *bidai* over it. On a hot and windless day, the rice is winnowed. The *bidai* is opened and the rice transferred to a series of circular baskets *(baka')* made of plaited rattan averaging about one bushel in capacity. The basketful of rice is taken onto the porch where the winnowing is done. The bearer tilts the basket slightly allowing a steady stream of rice to pour over the lip onto the *tikai senggang* which have been spread to receive the rice. As one person pours the rice, another fans it with a winnowing tray rapidly up and down, blowing the empty husks away. As the rice collects on the *tikai senggang,* it is returned to the large *bidai* to await final storing.

Storage

The storing of the rice is done in the evening of the first full moon after the harvest and requires about three hours. The storage is an event of moment, for the sufficiency of the rice until the next harvest depends upon a properly observed ritual of storing. If the rice is handled carelessly or without respect, it will be offended and diminished far more rapidly than it should. If it is handled with reverence, it may actually *increase* in storage.

The senior active woman stores the rice in large bark bins. The symbolism of fertility marks this climactic event in the rice year, just as it has every other aspect. Seed was stolen from woman in one mythical account. Seed is handled by women in sowing. And it is woman who replaces seed in the family's womb of life.

To obviate the possibility of any untoward sexual play either natural or incestuous, male members of the storer's family are not permitted to pass the rice up to the woman. Rather, a male from another family hands up the circular baskets *(baka')* or half husks of coconut *(tachu')* in which the rice is moved from *bilik* to loft.

As in all stages of the farm year, storage is observed with offerings. After the rice has been poured into the bins, it is stamped down to make certain that none of the rice is wasted. After the bins have been closed they cannot be opened until the next waxing of the moon. To do so would invite a magical loss of the rice. When the bins are opened, popped rice is scattered over the rice to ensure the favor of the rice soul. The principal woman worker then takes a coconut husk and gently gathers the rice that is to be removed. The rice is transferred from the husk to a circular basket to be taken to the verandah for husking.

Throwing Off the Pollen

After all of the families in the longhouse have completed storing their rice, one final festival, "Throwing Off the Pollen," is observed. Offerings are made to the gods and spirits, and members of the community join in a communal meal of rice beer, cakes, and other food. The purpose of the festival is to mark definitively the completion of all farm work for another year, and to demonstrate ritually that the people are not handling rice any more that year, so that the irritants of the rice will not cling to the workers and make them sick.

Husking

Rice is husked in most hill communities with a mortar and pestle, or alternatively with a two- or three-piece wooden mill. Using the former technique, women pound the husks from rice in a wooden mortar, shaped like an inverted commodore's hat, using a hardwood pestle about five feet long. Frequently women share in the husking of rice, three or four deftly raising their pestles in turn and bringing them down onto the rice that is poured into a small circular depression in the center of the mortar. In some communities the mortars are attached to sounding boards, so that the otherwise monotonous job produces a pleasant resonant beat which can be heard for several hundred yards.

When women use the wooden mill, rice is poured into the top of the mill and falls through a hole onto notched grooves atop the lower section. Holding a handle on either side of the upper section, a woman twists the mill back and forth so that the husks are separated as they are forced over the notches of the grooves, falling with the rice into a basket below.

The minimum requirement of husked rice is about one pint per person each day. By the early adolescent years, youngsters eat as much as their parents. The husking of rice, therefore, is usually done once a day, and a family's requirements are prepared at one husking.

Rice is rinsed once, to wash away any dirt, small stones, or other impurities. In cooking, the water level is about the width of two fingers above the rice, which is never stirred after being put into the pot and over the fire. After it is boiled, the rice is removed from the pot with either a wooden spatula or large metal spoon which is drawn across the rice, rather than being plunged straight into it, in an effort to preserve the separateness of each grain. Rice is eaten with salt, saltfish, and jungle vegetables, some of which we consider next, and is always handled with the right—i.e., the clean and "smart"—hand.

SUBSIDIARY ACTIVITIES

Next to rice cultivation, the most important forms of adaptation have been collecting and fishing. These are universal activities through which the Iban have acquired food as well as items for trade.

Rice is complemented with a variety of jungle vegetables, collected both by men and women for consumption with the evening and morning meals. Edible ferns such as *paku'* and *kemiding* are gathered, the stalks being broken off about six inches below the tip and cooked with chilis. Bamboo shoots are cut out, cleaned, sliced, and boiled. The cabbages of several species of palm, including the sago, nipa, *pantu', maram, lalis,* and *bindang,* are cooked similarly and range in taste from almost bland to bitter.

Iban customary law provides that anyone may eat the fruit of another person's tree at the tree, but it is a violation subject to fine to remove the fruit from that place. Sarawak abounds in fruits, most of which are eaten raw. The most important fruits in the Iban diet are the jackfruit, rambutan, durian, and *lensat.* Others that vary from one community to another include the several species of bananas, plantains, mango, mangosteen, papaya, guava, Malay apple, water apple, oranges, pomelo, star fruit, and soursop. The durian deserves a special note, and the reader is urged to see the remarkable description of this fruit in the *Encyclopedia Britannica.*

Numerous species of bamboo and other large grasses are collected by both men and women for a wide variety of purposes. Bamboo provides material for water containers, calabashes, flooring, and walls. Reeds are woven into baskets and mats by women as a "spare time" activity. There is a continuous demand for these items so that a regular production for replacement is essential. Mats are used for covering the floors when sitting and are rolled up when not in use lest they be soiled by the dogs. Baskets serve many uses, including their function as containers for seed, harvested rice, jungle produce, and personal effects.

Next to rice, aquatic life provides the principal source of protein in the Iban diet. Iban techniques of fishing are highly sophisticated and are adjusted according to water conditions. Fish traps are placed in constricted streams. In larger streams and rivers the seine-net is cast from the bow of a dugout. When tributaries flood, nets are stretched across the streams with an incline of about 20° from the upriver side so the fish will become entangled as they move downstream.

A large catch of fish in remote areas poses a problem of consumption and storage. Lacking facilities for refrigeration, the Iban have solved the problem in several ways. A portion of the fish is consumed immediately. Part is cubed and stuffed into lengths of fresh-cut bamboo to be parbroiled over the hearth. Two or three days of slow parbroiling over a low fire produces a succulent fish that is unexcelled in tenderness and flavor. If the catch is very large, most of it will be pickled. The Iban dice the fish, salt it well, and pack it away in earthenware crocks to "ripen." After one or two months the crocks are opened, and the pickled fish *(jukut, kasam)* is eaten as a condiment by those who made it or sold to other communities.

Animal Husbandry and Hunting

As a general rule the livestock kept by the Iban is either for ceremonial occasions or for marketing. Little is consumed in their daily fare. A chicken may be killed to honor a guest or a pig for a festival. Cockfighting provides a time for friendly competition and betting in which the roosters that lose end up in the pot. Rarely, however, is a fowl or animal killed for consumption by members of a single family.

The Rejang River below Sibu as it twists and divides on its way to the South China Sea.

A bard (*lemambang*) invoking the god Sempulang Gana and his attendants during the Festival of the Whetstones (*Gawai Batu*). The pig he carries will be sacrificed, its liver excised and the ventricles read. (Photograph courtesy of Richard Schwenk.)

(Above) Clearing secondary jungle for farm. Secondary jungle is dense with creepers, shrubs and small trees in contrast to more shaded and clearer space in primary forests. (Courtesy of Richard Schwenk)

(Left) Firing of farm site. Dense smoke indicates wetness of limbs and leaves, making for an imperfect and incomplete burn. (Courtesy of Richard Schwenk)

(Below) Fire after four weeks of dry weather. Burn was much more complete than at farm in previous picture.

(Above) Rice farms slope down to river. Imperfect clearing helps decrease erosion. In lower foreground man uses dibble stick as woman behind him sows. (Below left) Iban man uses dibble stick to punch holes into burned field to receive seed sown by women. (Below right) Even in areas where more acculturation has occurred, note man's clothes and hat, traditional patterns of sowing persist. (All courtesy of Richard Schwenk)

Harvesting *(ngetau)* is done by hand to avoid giving offense to the spirit of the rice. (Courtesy of Richard Schwenk)

Transporting rice from fields to longhouses is heavy work. Both men and women share in task. Harvest baskets may weigh up to 180 pounds when full.

(Above) man and woman at right fan woven winnowing piece *(chapan)* as women pour stream of rice to separate chaff from rice. (Courtesy of Richard Schwenk) (Below) Two women use hardwood poles as pestles to break husks from rice kernels in rice mortar.

(Above left) An Iban woman uses a rice-mill *(kisar)* to separate husks from kernels. After grinding rice in mill, she will winnow it using specially designed winnowing piece *(chapan)* just behind her. (Courtesy of Louis R. Dennis) (Above right) Iban man husks rice with gasoline-powered rice mill. (Richard Schwenk)

(Below) Iban woman cooks evening meal of rice and boiled greens over common hearth. (Louis R. Dennis)

(Above) Children swim in river before longhouse at Sungai Assan. Dugout in left foreground is most commonly used means of travel on small rivers.

(Below) Longhouse with areca and coconut palms, chicken coops in lower foreground.

(Above) Verandah *(ruai)* in longhouse which provides access from front of longhouse to family rooms.

(Below) Human skulls *(antu pala')* are hung in front of family rooms on verandah as trophies and signs of family's distinction. (Charles F. Root)

(Above) Numerous domestic tasks are performed on the verandah, from splitting firewood to removing the pith of cane to be used in weaving.

(Below) Iban woman weaves basket. Note difference in flooring materials in this and preceding picture.

(Above left) Verandah is play area for children during daytime when adults are in fields or away from the longhouse. Infants often sleep in sarongs suspended by spring from loft joist. (Above right) Responsibilities of children for younger siblings begin before adolescence.

(Below left) Few activities are done alone as Iban have selected for community, not privacy. Two friends fetch water together. Note containers which include plastic bucket and used acetic acid bottle (for treatment of rubber), and metal buckets. (Below right) Father with sickly child. Amulet was placed about child's neck and bamboo offering pieces fixed during healing ritual.

(Above) "A wandering conversation" *(randau ruai)* is a regular—almost nightly —feature of life in longhouse.

(Right) "The end of a longhouse"—an abandoned house showing deterioration and sections: loft above, family room to left, verandah to right. Rice-bins have fallen from loft above.

(Below) Iban girls carry "rice babies" *(anak padi)* in Festival of Transplanting *(Betambak)*. Even in areas where wet rice is cultivated, rice still is personified and given human attributes. (Richard Schwenk)

(Above) Wet rice fields. In right foreground, rice already has been transplanted. Working party transplants rice in center.

(Below) City of Sibu with *pasar* or trading center to right and residential areas in lower left. The Rejang encircles the island of Keretau in center of picture and divides to form Rejang and Igan at extreme right.

(Above) Traditional and modern meet in Sibu. Longboats—now equipped with outboard motors—and ocean-going freighter.

(Below) "God Save the Queen." Flags decorated streets on Queen Elizabeth's birthday, prior to Sarawak's entrance into Malaysia in 1963. Note advertisements.

Nuai, regal Malay lady, granddaughter of the Pengulu Dalam Munan, and cousin of Lemok Manggah.

Chinese women and children in quarters behind shophouses. Bamboo carrying poles are still used.

(Top) Heavy clay soils unsuitable for rice are excellent for pepper gardens.

(Above) Gunny sacks of processed pepper being moved to docks. (Below) Chicle soaking in pond before transporting to market.

(Above) Agronomist and Chinese tapper check flow of latex from cut on rubber tree.

(Left) Men clean area around secondary burial houses. Cemeteries must be given regular care lest spirits be antagonized and rice crops be adversely affected.

(Below) Iban widow reflects on past before husband's grave. Note articles *(baya')* given to help dead in their travels.

Almost all families keep chickens and pigs. In most upland communities the chickens are kept in rattan cages which are suspended from the underside of the verandah. Rice husks and mash are put into the cages by lifting one of the floor slats. Prized roosters are pegged alongside the apartment doors and are fed in half-shells of coconuts. Pigs roam beneath the long-house, feeding off the droppings that fall through the slats of the floor and the swill provided by the owners. In some communities pigs are penned in front of the house or immediately beneath it.

Hunting is a favorite diversion among men and boys, but the frequency of such activity varies from one community to another. Deer, wild pigs, anteaters, macaques, and gibbons are the principal animals hunted.

Dogs are kept in every longhouse, and traditionally have been important in hunting. Today, in many longhouses where hunting is infrequent, most families have at least one dog. (In one house I visited on the Igan River below Sibu, a family of five supported fourteen dogs who consumed what to me seemed an amazing amount of rice gruel, given the relative poverty of the family. I must admit in all honesty that my memory of the dogs in that house is somewhat tainted by my having awakened about three o'clock in the morning to find three dogs as my bedfellows on the verandah: one was at my feet, another by my waist, and the third was sharing my pillow.) Dogs roam over the verandah singly or in groups of two or three, their steps making a clatter of the loose slats. When their presence becomes annoying to the Iban, a well-placed kick or punch sends them yelping away.

Many families keep cats which prowl over the apartment walls and through the lofts in search of rats and other prey. Cats are usually much less noticeable than dogs in the longhouse.

Jungle Produce and Trade

In addition to the importance of subsidiary activities in the acquisition of food, the Iban for centuries have gathered forest products which they have exchanged with Chinese and Malay traders for beads, salt, iron, crockery, and the enormous earthenware jars found as heirlooms in every longhouse. Thus, any notion of the Iban as "primitive isolates" is a fiction. The

Iban long have been aware of regional demands, and within the past century, of world markets for their jungle goods. After the introduction of money, the sale of jungle products was important to the Iban because it was the single way they had of obtaining hard cash, whose value was quickly recognized.

Although we are getting slightly ahead of ourselves, by the beginning of this century Iban had begun the collection and sale of several items in addition to the exotica traded traditionally. Prior to the introduction of para rubber, a local natural rubber called gutta percha was the most important item of trade. When para rubber was introduced, gutta percha fell in price. The fall of gutta percha was compensated for, however, by the meteoric rise in the second decade of this century in the price of chicle. This rise coincided with the development of the American habit of chewing gum and is further illustrative of the ways aboriginal gatherers have been tied in to market systems abroad.

Rattans have been important as an item of trade since 1870. These canes are exported for the manufacture of furniture. Prices of rattans fluctuate tremendously, and when they fall the Iban stop cutting them, thus demonstrating their wisdom about market conditions.

Another natural product of occasional but unpredictable importance to both Iban and Chinese is the illipe nut (a seed of the various species of *Shorea*). Most of the crop comes from the hills of the Upper Rejang Valley. The seeds are a source of an unexcelled polyunsaturated fat and are exported mainly to the United Kingdom where the fat is used principally in the manufacture of chocolates and cosmetics. The Iban press the fat, which is molded into margarine-like blocks and eaten as a delicacy with rice.

The illipe nut is a highly unpredictable crop. Really heavy seeding occurs on an average of once in four years. Only a fortuitous combination of soft rains and gentle winds allows the nuts to set. More often heavy downpours and gusting winds destroy the flowers. When a heavy crop occurs, the Iban abandon all other activities and take to the forests to collect as many nuts as their boats can hold—sometimes, disastrously, more than they can hold. Hardly a season of illipe collection passes without some Iban overloading his boat and losing everything when it capsizes.

One further note about the importance of trade: over generations there has developed a symbiotic relationship between the Iban and other indigenes, as suppliers of forest products from the interior of Borneo, and the Chinese and Malays as professional traders, first on the coasts and recently up the major rivers. These relations, together with the attraction of the sparsely settled and productive areas of the plains, have been responsible for major changes in the lives both of those Iban who have moved to downriver areas, and to those who continue to live in the hills. As the Iban have become increasingly involved in non-traditional techniques and with non-Iban, their world has been enlarged and radically changed.

SUMMARY

The production of hill rice has been the central focus of Iban activities. Stretching over a ten-month period each year, rice farming has been the most protracted and elaborated of all activities. Scores of rituals exist to ensure success.

Although rice farming is the dominant feature of Iban adaptation, the Iban have remained dependent upon hunting, fishing, and collecting. While these activities provide up to 50 percent of the Iban's food supply and are especially important during the months "when the ladle hangs empty," they are considered less important than rice farming. This judgment is to be inferred from the total absence or minimal development of any rituals associated with the subsidiary activities, even though success is by no means certain.

Long-term coastal trade with Malays and Chinese has brought not only goods otherwise unavailable on Borneo, but contacts with peoples from other parts of Asia and an awareness of the existence of other societies even farther away. Trade of jungle produce was the initial form of interaction which served to orient the Iban to world markets and to the use of money.

Chapter 5

IBAN CULTURE

The Iban world was produced from an intense interaction between the Iban and their environment. This interaction both resulted from and led to a remarkable sensitization of the Iban to the natural, social, and metasocial domains. Characterized by a venturesome spirit, optimism, and individualism, the Iban have exuded confidence about their place in their world, which they have comprehended and symbolically structured.

From the ground up, the Iban has felt a part of his world. He identified with the land from which he came as "Molded Earth" *(Tanah Kempok)*. His life was inseparably tied to the land from which he received life and to the god of which—Pulang Gana —he regularly made his offerings. Man-land-god relations were ritualized in the acts of smearing earth on the forehead and of making libations to the soil upon moving into a new area in order to establish one's identity and to reintroduce one's self to the earth's owner. As we have seen in connection with Iban horticulture, reciprocity is a dominant theme in the numerous rituals.

In their sensitivity to every part of their world, the Iban have invested literally everything with the potential for sentient thought and action. This potential has resulted in a causality which embraces men, animals, birds, and even inanimate objects as agents. "Nothing happens without a cause," commented an Iban shaman, and in Iban lore, jars moan for lack of attention, trees talk, crotons walk, macaques become incubi, and the sex of the human fetus is determined by a cricket, the metamorphized form of the god Selampandai.

We have discussed the setting and migrations of the Iban. We have examined the organizing principles and settlement patterns of the Iban. We have analyzed Iban technology and rituals.

We now shall consider the ways in which the Iban become Iban, and the values which have been distinctive of their culture. By culture I mean the symbols which the Iban have developed experientially, which have ordered their world, made their lives meaningful, and constrained them to act in predictable ways. Iban culture has formed a bridge to understanding among its practitioners, and hopefully through this analysis a bridge may be provided for the non-Iban reader.

SOCIALIZATION

We have noted that children are highly prized by the Iban. At birth the infant literally becomes the center of attention—a fact important in appreciating the high esteem most hold of themselves. Infants are nursed immediately when they cry. The system of scheduled feedings is unthinkable, for as one mother said, "An infant's stomach doesn't count time." Infants and young children are rarely left by themselves. The young are held and fondled, carried on the back in a sarong, or when sleeping placed in a sarong suspended on a spring near one of the parents. Weaning is casual, and children of three to four years are suckled.

When the child is old enough he will be left by his parents, along with other children in the community, in charge of an older adult. The adult is available in case an accident occurs or a fight breaks out. The adult's supervision is of necessity casual and limited, for as soon as children walk they play over the verandah and porch, on the ground around the longhouse, and in the water if it is near the house and they have learned to swim.

Children quickly learn that threats of punishment are idle and meaningless, for only very rarely is a threat followed by action. Adults are permissive with their own children and with those of others, and a happy, relaxed relationship exists between sitters and their wards. In return for baby-sitting, older adults are given a part of the foodstuffs obtained by the children's parents.

Parents rationalize their indulgence of children, explaining that young children do not know anything and older ones resent parental interference. Parents also defend their easygoing ways in terms of the affection and support they want to win from the children. They dare not be harsh for fear no child will live with them and provide their living when they are old. On the other hand, children praise their parents for their patience. On the occasion of six different funerals, I heard children eulogize their parents with standardized expressions such as, "My father never scolded me" and "My parents never took their hands to me."

Of necessity brought about by the absence of parents during the daytime, children learn to fend for themselves at an early age. Older siblings take care of younger ones, help them out of scrapes, and "wipe their noses." Most children learn to cook, or to at least boil rice, by the age of ten. Parents wash the clothing of the very young, but by age seven or eight, children begin to assume responsibility for washing out their own few playclothes, and eventually every individual washes his clothes when he bathes. Through such commonplace activities children early learn the necessity and value of independence.

The absence of physical restraint and the assurance of approval of most of his activities encourages the Iban to be a confident and self-reliant individual. No greater offense can be committed against an Iban than shaming him. Members are well aware of the "face game" (Goffman, 1967) and learn means both of avoiding speech and actions which may shame another person, as well as defenses for rationalizing any feelings of guilt or shame which may be inflicted upon them.

Among children there exist hierarchical structures in which alliances are formed between more dominant ones. A considerable amount of teasing and scolding takes place and serves to develop defenses as well as to immunize children against rebuffs and criticism. Teasing is a major type of hostility release. When asked why a group of teenagers incessantly teased one of their group, a young girl replied, "There is no fun if we aren't teasing someone." But teasing is kept in bounds so that in-group teasing helps to define statuses and to strengthen the sense of solidarity of the young. This solidarity supports the child against adults, and he finds that the opinion and goodwill of his peers, with whom he spends most of his time, are to be more highly valued than those of his parents. Parents in turn hesitate to assert themselves for fear of alienating their children.

FAMILY AND FRIENDS

From childhood onward, sibling relations are marked by affection and mutual support. Siblings are often members of the same play groups which at younger ages are undifferentiated by sex. Brothers and sisters play chase, cross-catch, collect fruit, and fish together. By age eight, girls tend to play house and to pursue other more feminine activities, while boys perfect their hand-eye coordination by throwing stones and homemade spears, and by engaging in contests of topknocking.

Dancing is a favorite pastime. Children begin to practice the traditional *ngajat* as early as age five, and many quickly develop a proficiency of which they are vastly proud, "reluctantly" performing for visitors or on festive occasions. These performances by even the young reinforce the confidence of Iban children who are enthusiastically applauded by adults.

Since those who play together stay together, the recreational activities of Iban children are important in cementing sibling relations. The Iban are highly individualistic, yet there is an intense loyalty between siblings which lasts even after *bilik* partition. Older brothers and sisters who farm or have left the longhouse and are earning wages commonly feel responsibilities for and support their younger siblings.

This feature of sibling unity endures throughout the life of the Iban. Enchul, a farmer and entrepreneur of Rumah Gaong, once talked about staking his brother with money on three separate occasions to open his own shophouse. Each time his brother lost his business because of his own poor management. Knowing how critical and straithanded or miserly the Iban can be with one another, I asked Enchul why he continued to help his brother. Enchul replied with a mixture of annoyance and astonishment, "Even if I wanted not to help him, he's my brother."

The ideal of sibling unity is important among friends as well. Good friends frequently call one another *madi'*, and new acquaintances express their willingness and desire to become friends by use of the same term.

The apparently relaxed attitudes which mark parent-child relations conceal a number of tensions which exist among these adjacent generations of Iban, as they probably exist among all people. Iban parents despair over their willful children, but "the child is father to the man," and Iban children order their conduct according to the patterns of behavior which they have observed and learned from infancy. In a very real sense, children relive the lives of parents, and parents resent seeing their children become individualistic—as they themselves are.

Intergenerational conflicts are a recurrent theme in Iban oral literature—probably revealing the intense anxiety Iban feel about such relations. In the legend, *Kumang Lays Eggs (Kumang Betelu')*, there are a number of Oedipal connotations. The god Keling notices his wife, Kumang, surreptitiously laying eggs in a rice-bin (note the symbol of the womb). Angered and embarrassed by the act of parthenogenesis—and perhaps afraid that the female of the species *can* conceive on her own—Keling takes his spear, a patently phallic symbol, and pierces each of the seven eggs Kumang has laid. As he thrusts his spear into each of the eggs he does not kill the children but rather pierces their eyes, visually emasculating each of them. ("If your eye causes you to sin, pluck it out.") Keling now is burdened with seven blind sons who are dependent on him. Unable or unwilling to care for them, Keling takes his sons into the jungle where he loses them. Ambivalence toward father is expressed in two meetings with *Antu Gerasi Papa'*, the "Giant Spirit," a father figure. Blinded, the boys do not recognize the first spirit for what he is. He gives an unguent to them that restores their sight. With eyes wide open, they recognize the second spirit and kill him. After many perilous adventures, the sons return to their parents and are reunited with them. That such romantic endings do not characterize parent-child relations is obvious in light of *bilik* partition which in many cases may be traced to conflicts of interests between parents and adult children.

Figure 5. Terms of address.

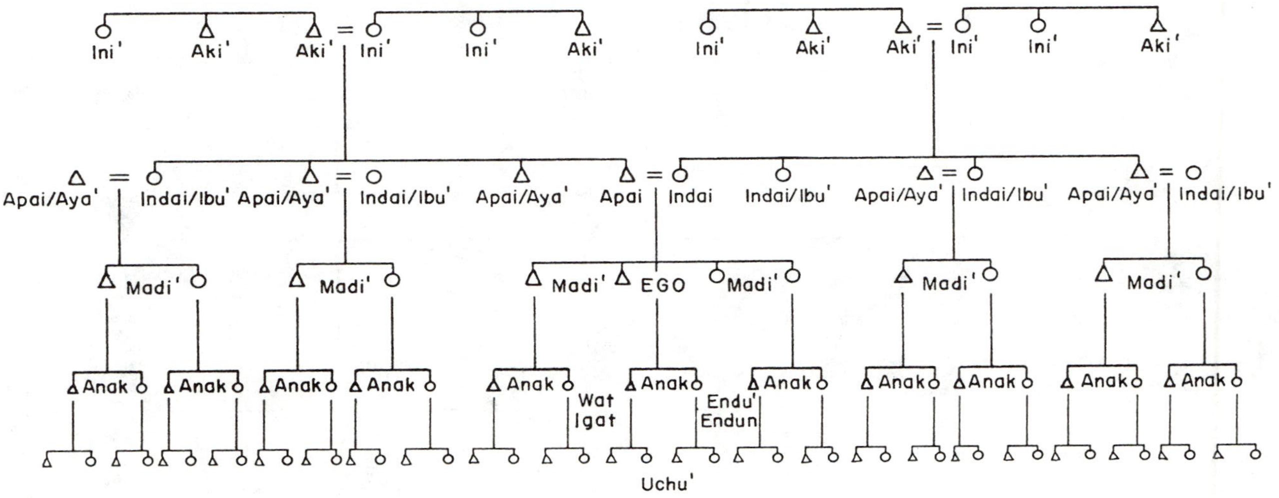

Figure 6. Terms of reference.

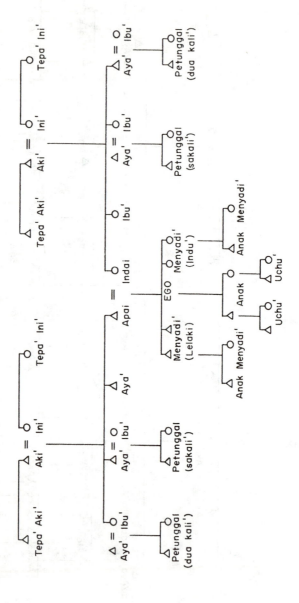

Figure 7. Affines.

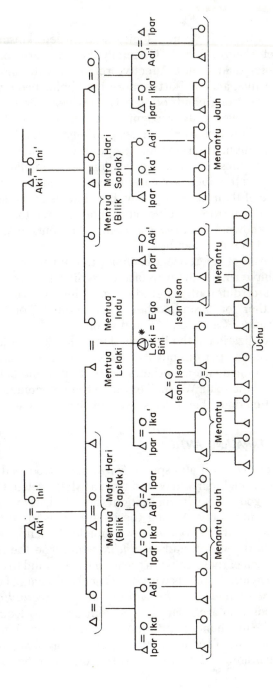

*Or, Apai Tuai / Indai Tuai, Lit. "Old Father" / "Old Mother"

97

Iban distinguish terminologically between kinsmen and affines (cf. Figures 5, 6, 7). Generally, kinsmen are considered to be closer than affines. Affective relations with kinsmen are more positive, and support is more readily forthcoming.

Although strong bonds often exist between affines, relations between in-laws are also recognized as tenuous at best, volatile at worst. "They just aren't our people," one man said of affinal relations, implicitly referring to differences between kingroups. The most problematic relation between affines is that of spouse and the siblings of parents-in-law. Iban practice name-avoidance of their parents-in-law, but siblings of the latter are considered to be most troublesome if not deferred to. Therefore they are known as *mentua mata hari*—"parents-in-law of the sun," or "too hot to handle."

Iban terms of reference are similar to the pattern of American kinship terms. Iban terms of address differ, however, in that members of different generations are "lumped" together as "grandfather" or "grandmother," "father/uncle" or "mother/aunt," "sibling," and "child," and so on.

The socialization of the Iban child includes not only an orientation to human persons but also to nonhuman personages who, although unseen, are nonetheless important in the beliefs and behavior of the Iban. We shall examine these nonhuman beings and the functions they have served in Iban adaptation.

PETARA AND *ANTU*

Gods *(petara)* and spirits *(antu)* are introduced to Iban children through narratives and drama. Myths relate the birth of various gods who, in turn, brought the world, its division, and life forms into being. Among the creator gods the most commonly known are *Seramugah,* who made the land, *Segundi',* who made the water, and *Segundit,* who made the sky. The name of each of these gods is a creation with a mind to euphony for each rhymes in chants with its particular domain of creative activity: *Seramugah, tanah; Segundi', ai';* and *Segundit, langit.*

The gods who are related to current activities loom larger and receive much more attention than do the creator gods. The most important of these functionary beings are *Sengalang Burong,* the brahminy kite, *Pulang Gana,* owner of the earth, and

Keling; although it must be noted that numerous other gods figure in the Iban pantheon, such as *Simpandai,* who gives birth to man, *Bungai Nuing, Pungga',* and *Bungai Laja'.* That the first three are more important, however, is to be inferred from the greater prominence they enjoy in myth and ritual.

Sengalang Burong is the "ruler of the spirit world." He, his seven daughters, and their husbands lived in the prototypical longhouse. It was he, according to one account, who introduced rice farming, death rituals, and headhunting to the Iban. Sengalang Burong and his seven sons-in-law have been most important in Iban augury. While divination has included hepatomancy, specifically, the reading of pigs' livers, and analysis of dreams, Iban concur that nothing has been superior to the flights and calls of birds, stating that "nothing is better than 'talking' with the birds."

The sons-in-law of Sengalang Burong—*ketupong (Rufous piculet), kikih/embuas* (Banded Kingfisher), *beragai* (Scarlet-rumped Trogon), *papau/senabong* (Diard's Trogon), *bejampong* (Crested Jay), *pangkas/kutok* (Maroon Woodpecker), and *nendak* (White-rumped Shama)—are the messengers of the gods. Their flights are significant when they fly from the right *(raup)* or left *(mimpin).* Three species are given two names *(kikih/embuas, papau/senabong, pangkas/kutok)* because of the different cries they make. Iban undertake or terminate activities according to the flight patterns and calls of these birds.

Other birds also are included in Iban augury, but they have not been incorporated into the sacred structure to the extent that Sengalang Burong and his sons-in-law have. On one occasion I was in Rumah Imba when an owl lit on the roof of a family section. The owl alighting on a house at night is considered to be a portent of death, and the Iban immediately began preparations for offerings to the spirit represented by the owl. At eight o'clock on the following evening the heads of the twenty-seven families in Rumah Imba gathered in the loft over which the owl had lit and put popped rice, rice cakes, and eggs into cane baskets. After the baskets had been prepared—three for each family: one to be hung at the top of the ladder leading from the *bilik* to the loft; one for the rear of the *bilik;* and one for the opening from the porch—a pullet was flung across the loft to the cry of, "There's an owl!" "No it's not," exclaimed the host, "it's only a chicken." Thus the owl and his spirit were faked off, as the Iban hoped by the ritual to lead the harbinger of death to believe that perhaps in fact he had not lit on that roof. If the minds of men can make gods of birds, then the minds of men are certainly capable of deceiving their "deities."

We have discussed Pulang Gana and his role in rice horticulture earlier. The Iban account for his ownership of the earth in several stories. According to one, Simpang-Impang, his mother, produced only blood as her first issue. The blood, which was thrown into a hole in the ground, became Pulang Gana and the earth his domain. In a second story, Pulang Gana followed a porcupine which had been raiding his underground garden. After a long chase, Pulang Gana emerged in the land of Seramugah, and after curing Seramugah's slave was given the youngest of the king's seven daughters for his wife. Thinking Pulang Gana dead, his family divided up all the property. As a gesture, when Pulang Gana returned, his eldest brother handed him a clod of earth saying, "It's too bad but this is all that's left, so it will have to be yours." Thus, Pulang Gana became owner of the earth, and when the Iban farm they acknowledge his ownership by invitations to rituals and sacrifices.

Beyond any doubt, the most popular if not the most important of the Iban gods is Keling. The accounts of Keling and his consort, Kumang, reflect the history of the Iban and are dynamic norms for behavior. The persistence of the Iban's belief in Keling, even among Christians, was demonstrated clearly when my nine-year-old son was accused of blasphemy at his suggestion to an Iban playmate that Keling was not for real.

Keling is the "collective representation" of what the Iban man should be. He is aggressive, proud, resourceful, brave, independent, and the bearer of tremendous personal magic. His travels are limited only by the number of his storytellers. Always in quest of adventure, he makes his way through difficult jungles, over flooded rivers, conquering human enemies and defeating the worst of evil spirits. He recapitulates Iban history. He is the Iban value system incarnate.

Keling is never in want, his farms never fail. His dress and equipment are the finest, his magic is all-powerful. Keling allows no obstacle to stand in his way. In one story he fights and dispatches a dozen different enemies, both spirits and human groups, and finally the entire army of the Malay king. As is evident, the story recalls much of the history of the Iban and their competition with other groups for land.

Kumang, like Keling, is also independent and resourceful. She appears in a slightly disadvantageous position by comparison with Keling, and it is well to remember that men have edited these accounts. For example, in one story Kumang violates a ritual prohibition against bathing—foolish female that she is—and as a result is lofted to the top of a giant citrus tree, requiring Keling and the other male-gods to undergo perilous adventures to rescue her.

If among the bivalent beings with which the Iban have peopled their world, the gods are positive examples to be followed, the *antu* are negative influences and things to be avoided. Whereas the gods are almost always benevolently inclined toward man, the *antu* are almost always malevolent toward them.

The *antu* probably are conceived in the matrix of hostilities, stresses, and antisocial tendencies with which the Iban, as do all people, have to deal. Belief in the *antu* serves the function of displacing the hostilities of the Iban onto a cosmic screen, whereas if the true "nature" of the *antu* were perceived and the hostilities directed against the real sources, community life would be disrupted. Living in a close community within sight and sound of one another, at a relatively simple level of technology, and in a jungle where on occasion even the most skillful of jungle people such as the Iban get lost, the *antu* are reifications of personal and communal problems and fears.

Intergenerational conflict is personified in the *Antu Gerasi Papa'*, the enormous, hairy, threatening figure. The *Bunsu Kamba'* stand ever ready to lead Iban into the jungles where they easily can become lost. *Antu Kelansat* is the "moocher" who feigns lameness and begs a ride of the unwary. Once he has climbed onto the back of the Iban, however, he refuses to dismount, clinging tenaciously until his victim collapses. The *Antu Kok-lir* is the spirit of the vengeful woman who has died in childbirth. Childbirth among the Iban, who lack a knowledge of germ theory and techniques of obstetrics, is dangerous; we have previously noted the high infant mortality rate. Deaths occur also to women in childbirth, and the *Antu Kok-lir* returns to eat the testicles of men, one of whose sex was responsible for her death.

Belief in the *antu* is a purposeful part of Iban education. Techniques in the educational process include stories about them, personal accounts of men and women who have "seen" them, and ritual dramatizations. One night in Rumah Usan, Menyan, a group of men and I were talking and some children were playing noisily nearby. Though they had been scolded several times, the children realized the emptiness of the adults' words and kept on with their play. Suddenly, one of the *bilik* doors burst open and out stepped an old woman in a long, tattered gown, wearing a frightening mask. The children were terrified and fled as one to the far end of the longhouse. When I asked the meaning of it all the people laughingly replied that the woman was playing *antu (Antu Muam)* in order to make the children respect the real *antu,* and observe behavior proper in the presence of adults and guests.

In the absence of other means of enforcing judgments and sanctions on dissident members, and in the situation in which every man might do what pleases him—anarchy resulting from full-blown egalitarianism—belief in the *antu* serves to give credence and authority to the scores of sanctions which provide guides to behavior. Through introjection of lessons about the *antu,* the Iban accepts their existence as a part of his behavioral environment. Belief in the *antu* is still universal, as is the notion that anything can become an *antu.* Consequently, though the Iban is confident and individualistic, he also is respectful and other-oriented, for fear that he may incur the wrath of the *antu* and bring their vengeance down on him.

Through interaction with human persons, and internalization of belief in nonhuman persons, the Iban learns a grammar of values which enable him to relate in predictable patterns with his fellows and to cope with his environment. This grammar of values admittedly is complex, but the following emphases stand out, subsuming a number of other themes. It is important to note that as these larger categories have developed to equip the Iban for survival in the hills, they have predisposed him to settlements on the plains and in urban settings as well.

SELF-SUFFICIENCY

The training of Iban children for independence, which we discussed earlier, is one facet of a larger value which we shall call self-sufficiency, or adequacy in the face of natural and cultural demands. Through the socialization processes, Iban children are instructed that they must be equal to the jobs that they are to take up. The first commandment for the Iban might well be, "Thou shalt measure up!"

Boys and young men are taught the skills and courage required of them to survive and support their families. For example, one of the technical skills that is expected of all Iban men is a high proficiency in the use of knife and axe. Iban children handle knives at age three or four—to the dismay of Western visitors, but with surprisingly few accidents—so that by late childhood they are able to perform the numerous tasks which require the use of a knife.

Young men learn to clear forests, build farmhouses, farm, fish, hunt, and distinguish the best types of trees for a variety of purposes, ranging from fire-laying to boatbuilding. Each is judged by the adequacy or excellence of his performance.

Likewise, girls and young women learn the roles which have been selected as appropriate to them. They help their mothers in cooking and serving food, caring for younger children, sowing and weeding the farms, collecting palm fronds and reeds for weaving, and gathering edible ferns, palm cabbages, and other wild produce. The woman is measured by her ability to feed and otherwise care for her family.

Self-sufficiency is particularly prescribed for rice farmers. It is in this area as in no other that the blessings of the gods appear. As we have noted, men who are successful farmers are sought out to pronounce blessings during agricultural festivals so that some of their good fortune may spread to others. In traditional Iban culture, though a man might be skilled as an augur, a shaman, or even a warrior, if the gods did not bless his farm, his ambitions foundered and he could not rise beyond this basic rung on the ladder of social ascendancy.

The Iban recognize that the family that enjoys good fortunes in the fields is also industrious. Abundant harvests are consid-

ered in part due to providence, but in large measure due to
hard work, as expressed in the following proverb:

> (You may have) one rice bin or two,
>   (Even) a magical hornbill stone,
> But if you do not attack
>   You won't fell the post,
>   And your manhood will be doubted.

> You may have one fish basket or two,
>   (Even) a magical whetstone,
> But if you do not go to your farm
>   You certainly won't get any rice.

There is a tendency for casual observers to lump entire communities together, dealing with them as homogeneous units. It
must be admitted that some communities are generally richer,
others generally poorer due to their location and history. Yet,
within every longhouse community there are differences in
abilities and persistence that are revealed in the basic value of
self-sufficiency. These differences emerge in discussions and in
the respect paid to individual members of the community.
Some may possess the tongues of angels with convincing speech
and facile expression, but unless their words are backed up by
performance, their credibility is quickly eroded. On the other
hand, quiet, unassuming men and women who farm well, develop their gardens, and know how to manage their affairs will
achieve respect and influence among their fellows. In their
evaluations of one another, the Iban are cruel critics of failure
and jealous respecters of success.

That some Iban do not achieve the ideal of self-sufficiency
scarcely needs stating. We have seen that less than one-half of
the families in our survey have enough rice to last from one
harvest to the next and therefore must supplement their crops
with loans from neighbors or subsist on substitute staples. At the
psychological level not all men approximate the ideal put forth
in the Keling narratives. Personality types range from the
strong, dominant male who is quite self-assured, to the trauma-
tized and sickly man, some of which type escape their conflict
through assumption of the shaman's role. In an interesting example of cultural irony, the shaman, who is unable to achieve
the norms of masculinity and "does not seek bravery" *(ukai*

ngiga' berani) as do other men, is the courageous one in bat-
tling the spirits and incubi before whom other Iban males pale
and tremble.

COOPERATION AND COMPETITION

Closely related to the major value of self-sufficiency and
personal adequacy are the two norms of cooperation and competition. Given the natural and social conditions to which the
Iban have adapted, cooperation has been essential to their
solidarity and survival, competition to their growth and expansion. The apparently contradictory nature of these two norms
disappears when we recognize that for the Iban they are not
antithetical but rather dialectical, requiring a maximum performance from the individual that in the end is to the benefit of
the group.

Competition cuts through all of the activities of the Iban,
even such "cooperative" ventures as house building, farming,
and partying. Comparisons are made of the size and quality of
materials of houses, yields of farms, and how many *more* people
came to the speaker's festival than to that of another community's. When I was talking with a well-known Iban of Kuching
about the hundreds of guests from thirteen houses who attended the *Gawai Antu* ("Festival of the Dead") at Rumah
Bebuling, Spaoh, in 1970, he replied with a wave of the hand
that it was nothing: "Why I had people from sixteen houses at
my daughter's recent wedding." And that was that.

"We Iban refuse to be defeated by one another," said Ganai
of Rumah Nyala. Just as kinsmen take pride *from* one another's
accomplishments, so too they are shamed by failures. For example, when the people of Rumah Nyala began construction of
their new longhouse in 1956, Ganai urged Machau, his brother,
to join him in collecting materials for construction of units in
the new house. Ganai told Machau that their family had never
lived in an unattached house *(pelaboh)* and that they should
build onto the new house. Machau replied that he was unable,
and as a consequence Ganai still feels a sense of shame even
though he himself built a unit on the longhouse.

Rice cultivation also is a highly competitive activity. When
families decide upon the size of their farm, they consider not

only their needs, the amount of land to be farmed, and the labor force they can muster, but also the size of their neighbors' farms and their anticipated relative yields. Competition is keen in such matters as the length of the workday. Keen competitors leave for the fields earlier and return later than others. Recalling the arm-breaking job of cultivating the soil in a wet-rice paddy, one Iban woman said that

last year, I farmed one acre next to a Chinese neighbor. We both went to our farms at daybreak. By three in the afternoon, I was ready to go home, but I refused because my neighbor was still working. I said to myself, "Later on you will have your fill, old girl." At five she quit, and I worked on until 5:30 to show her that I could.

The initiate's journey which we have mentioned is a highly competitive affair. Young men occasionally travel in groups, but the acquisition of goods and lore is done individually. As important as the travels themselves are, the men try to outdo one another in bringing back visible signs of their success.

Even the system of festivals which the Iban have developed, one of whose primary aims is the strengthening of solidarity within the "brotherhood," has provided a means for competition between members of the same and different communities. Hosts attempt to outdo one another in providing food and drink. According to Iban custom, if a guest is asked by a host to kill a pig, water buffalo, or turtle, he must reciprocate *in kind* when he hosts a festival. Shortly before the people of Rumah Nyala put on a festival, one of the members, Ambas, was able to buy a large land tortoise from some students who uncovered it in a drainage ditch. Ambas was euphoric, for several years earlier he had sacrificed a turtle at the festival of a friend whom he had been unable to repay and to whom he feared he was eternally indebted. To Ambas's immense delight, he presented the tortoise to his friend for sacrifice at the festival and the old account was settled.

In traditional Iban society the upward movement of men to higher statuses had to be ratified by giving festivals. Consonant with political processes in other societies at approximately the same technoeconomic level, Iban have had to create anew their statuses and to attain them through personal performance. Thus there was an emphasis not upon the accumulation and retention of property, but rather upon the acquisition of property and its distribution in order to acquire political capital.

Competition has encouraged a self-serving individualism which has been exploited by the Iban for the good of society. Pioneers made a name for themselves and enhanced their posterity, while at the same time opening up new areas for the less venturesome. Headhunting permitted the acquisition of trophies and recognition by the brave, and made possible the expansion of other Iban into the territories of the vanquished. Success in farming gained notoriety and power for the farmer, while ensuring that less skilled and industrious farmers would survive.

The Iban are rightly known as a highly individualistic people (cf. Freeman, 1955: 10), but their individualism is usually "in bounds." Iban speech is seasoned with expressions emphasizing the subjugation of the individual to the group. We have noted the independence of individual and *bilik*-family, but in matters concerning the entire community, personal independence and *bilik* autonomy are subject to the group's decision. I frequently have observed the Iban refuse to make any personal decision, deferring rather to "the meeting of the group" *(aum bala mayoh)*. And after a decision has been made through community discussion, members are expected to accept and to follow the consensus. To subvert the community decision is considered the height of treachery, and is compared to the story of the river fish, which, having completed a nonaggression pact with the crane, slyly bit off the crane's leg when he came to the water to drink.

Community solidarity and cooperation are more valued than individual success. On several occasions I observed a member of a community set himself up against the group, arguing against a community decision or criticizing the results of some previous action. Other members politely but firmly reproved him, using some appropriate proverb to the effect that the group was more important than the individual, goodwill more important than having his say. For example, the following proverb was used on one such occasion:

> The chicken has died, don't criticize.
> The spur has broken, don't make a fuss.
> The knife has broken, don't say anything.
> The shortknife has snapped, don't argue about it.

If the member does not accept their gentle rebuff and continues to remain obstreperous, members may quote any number of proverbs to the effect that he is more stupid than the group by setting himself against it—for the community will persist, while the individual will perish.

> You say that Malau is stupid, but it is you who
> are foolish and short-sighted.
> You say that I am silly, but it is you who are
> utterly senseless.
> You call yourself the Keling of heaven,
> But you are the Keling of "the opposite" *(Sebayan)*.

EGALITARIANISM

Precisely because there are some Iban who are more capable than others, who are keener competitors and whose achievements outstrip others, there is a strong emphasis upon egalitarianism. By egalitarianism, I mean the myths and rituals which support the ideal of personal equality vis-à-vis others, so that each person has the right to make his own decision, to speak his own mind, and to follow his own course of action.

It is through this value that the achievement orientation, so strong among the competitive Iban, is "reined in." By techniques subtle and obvious, individuals are kept in check lest they outdistance other members of the community. Leveling processes in the longhouse community have been among the most important pressures for conformity and consideration.

A delightful folk tale, universally familiar to Iban children, emphasizes the virtue of sharing equally regardless of size or ability. Long ago all animals went fishing (hence, the name of the tale, *Jelu Nubai*). The tapir was chairman and directed the activities. On each of the first four days the catch was large, but an *antu* came, frightened off the guards, and devoured the fish. On the fifth day, the tortoise and mousedeer were given the job of guarding the catch. The other animals thought that the two of them would be killed by the *antu*, but by stealth the two killed the *antu*. After they had enough fish, the animals gathered to divide the catch. The tapir gave the tortoise and mousedeer the smallest shares, saying, "Large shares to the large animals and small shares to the small," from which the Iban take the common expression, *pedua' badak,* "the division of the tapir," or *mit kelikit, besai kelikai,* "to the little, little, to the large, much."

The mousedeer and tortoise were peeved by the injustice. On the way home, the other animals made them paddle the boat while they slept. The two took fish scales and put them over the eyes of the other animals, after which they shouted, "The enemy is coming, the enemy is coming." The other animals, awakened but unable to see because of the fish scales, jumped into the water, leaving all of the fish to the mousedeer and tortoise.

In addition to this and other stories, numerous proverbs such as the following stress the value of egalitarianism and justice:

> Let the law be equal for all,
>> Just as a bushel measure is the
>> same for everyone.
> Do not ask some to climb the
>> thorn tree *(nibong)* and others
>> to climb the smooth betel *(pinang)* tree.

Through lore and example the Iban find that it is most judicious to do their own work and let others do theirs, offering few or no suggestions lest they be accused of impugning the abilities of others. "He knows more than others," or "he wants to make himself more than he is," are stinging Iban remarks which cut a person down to size.

In inter-*bilik* affairs, the Iban soon learn that to intrude in the affairs of another family is to invite trouble. In a popular child's story, "The Macaque's Tail" *(Iko' Kera'),* a group of macaques descended on a tree trunk that a man had been splitting before returning home to his lunch. One macaque was more mischievous than the others, shaking a wedge back and forth until it popped loose catching his tail in the crack. The man, hearing the cries of the macaque, ran back and killed it. "And such is the end of everyone who interferes with the business of others," concludes the moralistic story.

Pressures to make everything and everyone equal, or nearly so, have been important in the *gawai* or festival system. Of him to whom much has been given has much been required. As we discussed in the last section, distribution, not retention, is virtuous.

The commandment, "Thou shalt succeed," is tempered with the qualification, "but not too much." Understandably, therefore, the Iban can be both proud and humble, confident and uncertain, self-asserting and self-effacing. Children are taught to walk over the verandah without making unnecessary noise, lest they evoke the anger of adults. Passing in front of others, the Iban bows with palms pressed together between his knees to show his deference. Women learn to sit on their heels, men with their legs crossed in front of them, avoiding any appearance of arrogance.

When called upon to speak at a festival, the Iban must choose his words carefully, hedging his remarks with an apology, first for his inability to speak well, and second for anything wrong that he may say. Having covered himself in this fashion, he then proceeds to demonstrate that he is in fact equal or superior to his listeners.

MOBILITY AND OPPORTUNISM

Related to the strong achievement orientation and individualism of the Iban are two closely associated values: mobility and opportunism. The physical mobility of the migratory Iban is paralleled by a readiness to appropriate new techniques, names, and ideas *when* and *if* they are convinced acceptance is to their advantage. The ease of acceptance new members enjoy in a new longhouse is similar to the willingness the Iban have shown to take in foreign objects and concepts.

While I by no means want to imply that the Iban have traditionally rejected their own culture in favor of alien novelties, I do want to make clear that the Iban have not been intimidated by the new or strange artifact or symbol.

We have considered the physical mobility of the Iban. This is exemplified in their history of movements northward through Borneo, in the initiate's journey, and through pioneering. The festival *(gawai)* system required occasional and regular visits between kinsmen and friends.

Nor should we get the notion that the Iban were "stick-in-the-muds" who moved about only in the relatively small confines of western Borneo. By the beginning of this century, they were off to other parts of Southeast Asia and even Oceania. Tuba, a Bawang Assan bard of renown, has shared with me his adventures working in West Malaysia and—having completed his contract there—in the coal fields of New Guinea.

Adoption and the readiness of families to give or exchange children oriented members to both lasting and transient relations. The relatively high incidence of divorce, which could be initiated by either husband or wife, was related to the ability and even the willingness to break off old relations and begin new ones.

The Iban language is replete with loan words, most notably Sanskrit, which are of such antiquity that their users consider them part of indigenous speech. We have discussed the term *juru,* part of the names of the kin-group, as deriving from Sanskrit. Indeed, the generic name of the gods, *Petara,* is borrowed from the name of the Indian *Pitarah.*

Foreign items have been readily accepted, both for their utilitarian benefits and their aesthetic qualities. Chinese ceramics, particularly large jars selected for family treasures, were readily accepted, and in more traditional communities still serve as indicators of wealth and status. Some families have outstanding collections of Malaysian brassware—tobacco and betel boxes, lampstands, and delicately inscribed trays. The introduction of the shotgun produced a surfeit of owners in the early part of this century, as witnessed by the licenses in the Sibu District Office.

By opportunism I mean a tendency toward measuring decisions according to the relative advantages that the Iban anticipates. Thus some are inclined to seize the opportunity of the moment, regardless of ramifications of their actions. This ethic of expediency is understandable in light of the historic background of the Iban who have wrestled with an unpredictable environment and have been conditioned to seize immediate opportunities, for example, a break in the weather when a field can be burned, or suffer the consequences.

We shall defer further discussion of these values until the final chapter.

LUCK

The final value in Iban culture which we shall consider is a complex of attitudes which I classify under the heading, "luck." By luck I mean "the imponderabilia of life," both good and ill, which are fully felt but little understood. In the vagaries of nature to which the Iban have adapted and over which they have little effective control, luck has come to mean those events which sometimes are perceived as good, sometimes bad, but over which the individual or group are thought to have almost no power.

Good luck is the *summum bonum* according to a majority of Iban questioned. It is the value placed above all others, and blessed is the man on whom it falls. Good luck is the clearest and most certain sign of the favor of the gods. It is evident in success and achievements, and the blessings of the man who has luck are sought on festive occasions. The man with luck harvests bountiful supplies of rice each year. Formerly the man with good luck was in the right place at the right time, so that he performed acts of bravery and took human heads.

Despite the importance attached to luck and the lack of scientific explanations for much that happens in their lives, the Iban are by no means passive about their fates. Rather, they have developed, as we have seen, an elaborate complex of beliefs and rituals through which they attempt to manipulate their circumstances to their benefit.

Gods are conveyors of good luck. If given proper respect and treatment, the gods will be benevolently inclined. Sengalang Burong and his son-in-law give directions for all important events: taking a trip, planning a raid, planting a farm, or choosing the site for a new house.

Antu, on the other hand, are held responsible for many of the misfortunes that befall the Iban. An old man suffers a stroke—assault by an *antu.* A young child contracts gastroenteritis—passed by an *antu.* A mother has difficulty in delivery—the passage must be blocked by an *antu.*

Believing that nothing happens by chance, the Iban seek casual explanations for everything that occurs and attempt to guard themselves against misfortune. Medicines *(pengaroh)* and charms *(engkerabun)* are commonly used. Carved wooden figures stand like sentries to guard the approach to longhouses. Small huts contain offerings to divert *antu*. Amulets are tied around the necks of children to ward off *antu*-borne illnesses.

It is difficult, if not impossible, to convey the high degree of Iban ritualization aimed at ensuring good luck. We have noted the rituals connected with farming. A hierarchy of rituals exists to be performed by the shaman. Depending on the house and the way rituals are categorized, more than two dozen rituals are observed for the individual in his passage from womb to tomb, beginning with a blessing entoned as a rooster is waved over the new infant, and climaxing in this life with the "Hornbill Festival" *(Gawai Kenyalang)*, in the next with the "Festival for the Dead" *(Gawai Antu)*.

The building of a new longhouse involves more than a dozen rituals of varying importance, commencing with auguries taken at the site *(Ngabas Taba')* and concluding with the "Festival of the New House" *(Gawai Rumah Baru)*. The notion of luck is built into the orientation of the longhouse which must be built parallel to and fronting on its water supply; to turn one's "back-side" to the water would be unthinkable. The house must be constructed so that the course of the sun cuts right across the width of the house rather than running its length, lest the house be "hot and unhealthy" *(angat)*.

SUMMARY

The culture of the Iban has provided powerful symbols reflecting the intense interaction between the Iban and their environment and reinforcing the optimism and expansive tendencies of the most aggressive group in Sarawak. Encouraging competition, individualism, and achievement, the drives to achievement have permitted the individual to engage in self-serving activities which have also been of benefit to the group. The confidence engendered through the enculturation experience has made the Iban the most responsive of the indigenous peoples to the presence of other people and their values.

Chapter 6

ON THE PLAINS

Movements onto the plains of the lower and middle Rejang Valley exposed the Iban to conditions unlike those in the hills. These conditions, both natural and social, have led to numerous responses and changes at every level of their lives.

Below Kanowit, the Rejang Valley is bordered by vast plains and swamps, dotted with low-lying hillocks. Such higher land has been chosen for house sites, being safe from the waters that spread over the plains in time of flood and also being more accessible to cooling breezes. Close to Rejang, however, the land is flat and often higher ground in areas large enough to cultivate is inadequate or far away. Settlement on the plains required Iban to shift from the cultivation of hill rice to wet rice because of the combination of higher water table and flat lands. Alternatively, they can farm dry rice at considerable distances from their homes, as indeed some more conservative Iban do.

The arrival of the Iban in the Rejang Valley coincided with the extension of Brooke rule over the area, and preceded only shortly the immigration of thousands of Chinese. At about the same time, Malays moved into the valley from the coasts. The confluence of these groups has had marked effects on the members of each. Iban and Malay alliances have been particularly important in trade, warfare, hospitality, and ethnic evolution. The Iban have accommodated to the enterprising Chinese whose ways they often have emulated, albeit unwittingly. The Iban have acquiesced to Brooke, British, and Malaysian administrations which have radically reoriented them politically.

The introduction of para rubber—following the theft of rubber nuts from Amazonia in the nineteenth century—and participation in a monetized economy have led the Iban to redefine their concept of "work." Together with pepper gardening, the investment of time and energy in the development of rubber gardens has been of both economic and cultural significance to the descendants of former shifting cultivators. These activities have led to a diversification of incomes from resources in greater demand than jungle products and to participation in the trade of market towns.

Ideologically, traditional Iban values have been reinterpreted and in some cases abandoned. Changes in beliefs and rituals have been directly related to the new habitat, to greater technical control of productive activities, to increasing contract and involvement with non-Iban whose values are different from those of the Iban, and to continuing efforts to reconcile traditional and modern life-styles.

PEOPLING OF THE REJANG VALLEY

Before we describe technical changes among the downriver Iban, we shall consider the people of the Rejang Valley and other ethnic groups with whom the Iban have interacted and through whom many of the technical changes have been introduced.

The Melanaus

Originally, the Rejang was home primarily to a scattered population of Melanaus and Segalangs in the delta region, Kanowits, Beliuns, and Tanjongs in the middle Rejang, and Kayans, Bukitans, Lugats, and others in the upper Rejang. The Melanaus shared certain similarities with the Kayans, with whom they entered into aristocratic intermarriages.

Early contacts between the Melanaus and Malays were in the lower reaches of the rivers, the Malays not venturing far upriver. The Brunei Malays established their positions through intermarriage between Brunei nobles and the daughters of

Melanau chiefs, in time supplanting the Melanau chiefs and developing an aristocratic class whose descendants still live in many of the coastal areas.

The Melanaus of the middle and lower Rejang were still long-house dwellers and relatively untouched by the Brunei Malays and Islam at the time of the Iban invasions of the Rejang. Iban legends recount the struggles between their heroes and Melanau war leaders, such as the awesome Tugau whose sneeze in Sibu was heard at Nanga Retus some twenty miles down the Igan River. The Iban drove most of the Melanau from the Rejang, the only Melanau settlement in what is now the Sibu District being a small village at Kampong Nangka on the Igan River. Although the Melanaus have maintained their ethnic identity, in the area of the Rejang they have been substantially Malayanized.

The Malays

The Malays were a coastal-dwelling people, engaged in fishing and trade. Many lived in a symbiotic relationship with inland people, such as the Iban, exchanging salt and saltfish for rice, sago, and valuable jungle products which they traded to Chinese who made occasional calls at port towns.

With the advent of Islam, the spread of activist attitudes, and examples of political control, the Malays extended a network of trade relations from Brunei to Tanjong Datu. The Malays were not oriented to territorial domination but rather to the control of strategic river mouths.

Malays entered the Rejang Valley from the west at about the same time the Iban invaded from the south. According to Benedict Sandin, former curator of the Sarawak Museum and an Iban scholar knowledgeable of the period under discussion, strong alliances were formed between the Saribas-Skrang Iban and Malays—to the mutual advantage of both groups. In league with the Malays, Iban warriors found a legitimization for their raiding activities. Booty and captives were shared, with this assimilation of captured members of other ethnic groups ultimately contributing to the growth of Malay and Iban populations.

The invasion of the Rejang opened new lands not only to the Iban, but also to the Malays. That the Iban have considered the

Sarawak Malays as partners, at least in principle, is evident in their use of the term *udong* ("brother") for Malays to whom their families are allied, and in the oral literature of the Iban, especially in the folk tales of Apai Salui and Suma Umang.

Apai Salui, who personifies "the father of stupidity," represents negative characteristics which have adversely affected the fortune of the Iban and thus should be avoided. Suma Umang represents the Malays whom the Iban feel are a cunning people by whose craftiness they have been disadvantaged. One delightfully revealing story is related as follows:

Apai Salui lived in a large stone house and Suma Umang in a bamboo hut. Apai Salui had bins of rice and trunks filled with money. Suma Umang had nothing—except a split support under his hut through which the wind whistled.

One day as Apai Salui passed by, he heard the wind blowing through the support and was captured by the sound. "Friend," he said to Suma Umang, "let's exchange houses. You take my house of stone, with the bins, trunks, and other treasures, and I will take your hut." Without a moment's hesitation Suma Umang exclaimed, "Done!"

Apai Salui sat beneath the hut day after day listening to the wind as it blew through the support, until one day the wind blew stronger, the hut collapsed, and Apai Salui was crushed beneath it. But Suma Umang continued to live comfortably in the house Apai Salui had given him.

The Chinese

The first Rajah wanted to encourage Chinese immigration from which he hoped to derive the labor and income needed to build his state. However, little was accomplished during his rule, for he was too obsessed with extension of his territory and was almost bankrupt after the Chinese rebellion of 1857.

From his earliest days as an outstation official under his uncle, Charles Brooke, the second Rajah, saw the vast and largely untouched Rejang Valley as an excellent location for settlement of a Chinese colony. He shared the feelings of most Europeans that the indigenous peoples of Southeast Asia were not able to meet the labor requirements for economic development, and, further, he wanted to protect the Iban from the changes that such development inevitably would bring.

On November 29, 1880, Charles Brooke issued an order offering to negotiate with any Chinese company that would bring to the Rejang Chinese men, women, and children numbering not less than 300 people. The first Chinese settlers arrived at the fort-port of Sibu in 1901, a group of 603 Foochow who were followed the next year by 550 more of their dialect group. This was the beginning of movements involving eventually thousands of Chinese.

One of the expressed purposes for the Rajah's introduction of the Chinese into the Rejang was the cultivation of rice. The Rajah and his officials had long faced the problem of obtaining a cheap, local, and dependable supply of rice. They expected the Chinese settlers to be self-supporting in nine months, first producing enough rice and vegetables for themselves and then marketable surpluses. The first three years of the Chinese settlers were, to the contrary, disastrous. Many of the Chinese were not farmers and those who were found that the agricultural techniques used in China did not work well in the Rejang. Faced with shortages of food and mounting debts, the settlers quickly developed a wary disillusionment for rice farming.

One Chinese settlement had been established above Sibu, and its members quickly achieved success in growing pepper. Recognizing that greater rewards lay in pepper gardening, and motivated by the desire to eat daily, other Chinese turned first to pepper and by the end of the first decade of this century to rubber.

Ironically, the settling of several thousand Chinese among the Iban and Malays of the Rejang created conditions for change which the second Rajah avowedly had hoped to avoid. The land allocated for the settlers was not enough—at least according to the feelings of the Chinese settlers—and frequent Iban complaints of Chinese encroaching on their land were recorded. The Chinese notion of proprietary rights to land conflicted with Iban rights of usufruct, resulting in the establishment of a Lands and Survey Department by the Rajah and in the development of non-traditional attitudes to land among the Iban.

A willingness of Iban to sell their land to Chinese for the rewards of ready cash caused tremendous concern to the Rajah and his officers. A number of regulations attempted to remedy the situation but met with mixed success. Ultimately, Sarawak's land was divided into a Native Zone (from which the Chinese were excluded), a Mixed Zone (available to all citizens), and Crown land. Even today Chinese are restricted from holding or acquiring land in the Native Zone, but numerous ways of circumventing this restriction exist, such as the "adoption" of Chinese by Iban (for a price) thereby enabling the adoptee to obtain land in the Native Zone.

During the years of the expansion of rubber production—which we shall examine for its effects on the Iban—Chinese spread beyond their original settlements, planting rubber gardens and building small shophouses in locations accessible to rural residents. Because of the possible outbreak of violence, and the occasional incidents of headhunting still occurring, Chinese shops were located on the main rivers near the mouths of tributaries. There they commanded trade in and out of the tributaries while permitting escape if trouble erupted in the hinterland. Some trading centers grew to include several shops, for example, the Durin bazaar which includes about one dozen shops. Most important, Iban and other indigenes were increasingly involved in an expanding trade network which tied them into the village shophouse, and beyond that oriented them to trade in Sibu, Kanowit, and other *entrepôts*.

We now shall analyze the adaptive strategies of the Iban in the lower and middle Rejang where they have taken up new practices of subsistence in response to different natural conditions and cultural contacts.

WET RICE FARMING

The schedule of activities in wet rice farming is essentially the same as that for shifting cultivation, which we have described. The horticultural year begins at about the same time with an annual meeting to determine sites and to plan the Festival of the Whetstones, and concludes with the ritual storage of the harvest.

A comparison of the techniques employed and rituals observed by wet rice farmers does show a number of important differences from the practices of dry rice farmers. Recently these differences have become even more pronounced because of the proximity of wet rice farmers to the Agricultural Department and to Chinese merchants from whom they are able to obtain much more sophisticated equipment, some designed specifically for the flooded padi fields. Some rituals have undergone editing, others have disappeared in the new context. For example, wet rice farmers ritually transplant the rice seedlings, paralleling in some respects the ritual planting of the sacred rice in the hills. These farmers no longer observe the rituals "Visting the Burned Site" and "Washing Off the Charcoal," which are peculiar to slash-and-burn horticulture.

We shall not repeat those features of rice farming that are duplicated in both areas, but instead discuss techniques and rituals that differ from hill farming and are peculiar to wet rice farming.

Clearing

The task of clearing lowland sites near the rivers and their tributaries is considered much easier than felling the large trees in virgin jungles or even removing secondary growth in the hills. Doubtlessly pioneers faced the same problems, but in present lowland farms the land is cleared with longhandled chopping blades *(pito)*, bushknives, and weeding knives. Because of the annual deposits of alluvium, fallow periods have not been as long and secondary growth not as thick. Although men join their wives in clearing the fields, their presence is not as necessary as it is in the hills where they must perform the heavier tasks. As we shall discuss later, this "freedom from farming" has been of crucial importance in the diversification of activities among downriver Iban.

Recently the government and private merchants have introduced pack sprayers and herbicides. The proximity of some Iban to the market towns of the Rejang and the availability of relatively cheap transportation, such as Chinese launches and buses, have permitted the Iban on the Igan and Leba'an rivers to purchase sprayers and chemicals to clear their fields. When pack sprayers are used, men do the spraying. Within two days after spraying, farms are rolled with fifty five-gallon drums partially filled with water, pressing the dead grasses and stubble into the soil. The decomposing material fertilizes and mulches the soil.

The Iban who farm wet rice enjoy a much greater freedom from the vagaries of nature than do their upriver peers. Particularly among the thousands who now are participating in the government rice planting schemes, they are able to farm the same sites year after year, obviating the necessity of contending with trees and undergrowth as well as any dependence on the short dry season which is so crucial to dry rice farmers.

Planting

Wet rice farmers sow their seed in beds which are made on relatively high, well-drained soil. Often the beds are some distance from the fields because of the topography of the area. In extremely low-lying areas some farmers make their rice beds in eight-foot squares of earth and ash about three inches deep on their covered verandah or uncovered front porch. This latter practice, however, is limited to those areas where the beds are liable to be flooded.

Rice beds are planted within two days of the first full moon in June. The moon figures prominently not only in the rituals but also in the ethnoscience of the Iban, who like the "old wives" in Western cultures are aware that different plant species respond differently to the light and phases of the moon.

The life/death motif noted earlier in the beginning and ending of life with rice appears in language associated with the rice beds. The seed are "entombed" *(dikubor)* that they may rise again and give new life to the planters. Subspecies of rice are planted in separate areas of the beds, so that they may be kept apart when transplanted onto the main fields—because of the different character and soul substance which each possesses.

To this point men and women may participate equally in the work, except that the task of making the rice beds usually falls to women. In the case of families whose men work elsewhere, almost all of the work of clearing and planting falls to women and their parents who may live with them. This assumption of the role of principal farm worker by women has led to a higher incidence of matrilocal residence among the downriver Iban, in contrast to the upriver Iban who are ambilocal.

Transplanting

When the rice shoots are about eight inches high, the sacred rice *(padi pun)* is transplanted and offerings are made to be certain that the shoots will be received in the soil that is strange to them. This ritual, which traditionally has included a libation of chicken's blood to the owner of the soil, Pulang Gana, is unfailingly observed and no other strain of rice may be planted until the sacred rice has been transplanted.

It should be noted that whereas the planting of the sacred rice climaxes the first stage of horticulture in hill farming, it marks the beginning of planting in wet rice farming. The transposition of this ritual in the schedule is related to the degrees of control in each area. In the hills, the sacred rice is planted after other varieties are sown *in order to* ensure their germination and the success of the farm. On the plains, the sacred rice is planted before other varieties are transplanted *because* it and the other varieties have germinated and the success of the farm must be acknowledged. This is not to imply that wet rice farmers do not face problems and uncertainties, but to indicate how they ritually have expressed the differences in natural conditions.

The "real" work of transplanting is marked with the ritual placing of a basket of rice seedlings at the farm site. Then the seedlings from the beds are brought to the fields by both men and women. In keeping with the feminine fertility theme discussed earlier, only women and girls perform the job of transplanting. The seedlings are taken from larger baskets, transferred into smaller baskets the women have tied around their waists, and individually planted into a hole gouged with a short stick.

The seedlings are transplanted into rows. When one strain is completed a new row is begun for the next, or else boundaries between the two strains are marked. A survey of sixty farms at Rumah Nyala, Aup, and Rumah Imba, Salim, showed that each farm contained an average of fifteen different varieties of rice, divided almost equally between those strains maturing in three months and those maturing in six months. The six-month varieties are planted between mid-August and the first of September, and the three-month varieties by the end of October.

A frequent practice involves leaving a strip of land three feet wide between the three- and six-month varieties. This strip is planted with vegetables, the species depending upon the quality and height of the land. The vegetables include most of those planted in upland regions, such as maize, Job's tears, eggplant, pumpkins, longbeans, mustard greens, and gourds. In some low-lying areas where it is impractical to mound up the soil or to leave such a strip, vegetable seeds are broadcast among the rice plants, the rationale being that the plant growth helps with weed control.

Weeding

Weeding begins as soon as the rice is transplanted. Ideally each farm is weeded once or twice more, according to the weed growth. Even in lowland areas weeding is done predominantly with the forked stick and weeding knife, the grass and other vegetation being pulled over and cut just above ground level.

Where resources permit and accessibility makes it practical, Iban may weed with the pack-sprayer and selective herbicides which kill the grasses but do not affect the young rice. This is a common procedure among the families at Rumah Nyala and other communities participating in rice-growing schemes.

Fertilizing

In contrast to the upriver Iban who depend almost entirely upon potash from the fired fields for fertilizer, the downriver Iban frequently make use of commercial fertilizers. Ninety of the 140 longhouse communities in the Sibu District are involved in government schemes through which the Iban have been encouraged to use urea, phosphates, and various ratios of chemical fertilizers. Small quantities are given free to participants in the schemes to demonstrate their usefulness, and fertilizers are for sale in more than a dozen shops in Sibu.

A majority of adult Iban are still illiterate, but many are able to recognize the chemical symbols and talk avidly about "N-P-K." Iban men sit on their verandahs mixing and measuring the quantities of fertilizer their farms will require.

The Iban have discovered, in addition to the benefits derived from fertilizing, some other, not too desirable, results. For example, during the agricultural year 1970–71, Ganai of Rumah Nyala spent almost $70 on fertilizers and labor hoping to produce a bumper crop. His rice responded to the fertilizers, but to his woe his neighbors were reluctant or unable to spend as much on fertilizers. His rice filled out earlier than that of his neighbors and despite his family's day-to-day guarding, Ganai alleged that sparrows and rats consumed almost one-half of his crop.

Guarding the Fields

The Iban of the lower and middle Rejang continue to practice the ritual tabooing of the fields *(Ngemali Umai)*. As we shall discuss later, thousands of Iban in this area have become Christians, but this ritual is observed almost universally, regardless of religious affiliation.

Techniques used for protecting the standing grain are basically the same as those described for hill farmers. In addition to the native devices, bits of metal and pieces of broken mirrors are attached to strings in attempts to frighten the birds.

The problem of pests varies from one area to another, and some years from one community to the next. Generally, Iban farming wet rice tend to be much less afflicted by pigs and deer than their upriver fellows, and more victimized by stem-borers, leaf-folders, and other insects.

The Lean Months

Only 36 percent of the Iban in our sample of four longhouses had enough rice from their harvests to last from one year to the next. When supplies run out, Iban in more remote areas must rely on the less than desirable rice substitute, sago, or if members of their community have surpluses they may be able to buy or borrow from them. We shall see that one of the *raisons d'être* of the longhouse with the emphasis on the individual family is to preclude the possibility of putting all of the rice into one bin.

By far the most successful farmers are those who cultivate strategically located promontories which are annually replenished with nutrients in the deposits of alluvium. Thus, at Rumah Nyala only thirteen of the thirty-three families did not have enough rice to last from one harvest to the next (see Table 6–1). At Rumah Gerasi, Melangan, below Sibu, yields for each of the years 1970–1972 were adequate for two years' supply of food, so that the Iban have been able to lay by bins full of rice and to sell much of their rice.

At Rumah Gaong, where many Iban still farm hill rice, only three of the thirty families had enough rice to last from one

Table 6-1 Acreage and rice yields, Rumah Nyala, 1970–1971

Bilik Number	Size Farm (acres)	Yield Rice (picul*)	Sufficiency (%)	Bilik Number	Size Farm (acres)	Yield Rice (picul*)	Sufficiency (%)
1.	2.0	14.0	100	18.	1.5	30.8	100
2.	1.5	26.6	100	·19.	4.0	56.0	100
3.	2.5	18.2	50	20.	1.5	8.4	30
4.	1.5	24.4	100	21.	1.5	21.0	100
5.	2.0	14.0	50	22.	1.0	7.0	30
6.	2.0	14.0	100	23.	1.5	19.6	100
7.	0.6	5.6	100	24.	1.0	14.0	100
8.				25.	2.0	15.4	40
9.	1.5	28.0	100	26.	1.0	9.8	30
10.	1.5	26.6	100	27.	1.5	24.4	40
11.	1.0	15.4	100	28.	1.5	14.0	80
12.	1.5	18.2	100	29.	0.3	2.8	30
13.	2.0	25.2	100	30.	1.5	18.2	100
14.	1.0	15.4	80	31.	1.5	11.2	40
15.	1.0	15.4	80	32.	0.5	5.6	60
16.	3.0	29.4	100	33.	2.5	28.0	100
17.	3.0	35.0	100				

*Picul = 133.33 pounds.

harvest to the next. Members of twenty families were hired from time to time by Enchul, the local shopkeeper, to plant his pepper gardens and clear undergrowth from around his rubber trees. Enchul not only has had a surplus of rice every year since moving to Rumah Gaong twenty years ago, but is a personal example of economic differentiation as he has maximized his advantage by providing rice in exchange for the labor of other members of his community who are in his debt and service.

In the case of Enchul, as in that of other emerging Iban traders, the few successful farmers have been able to take advantage of the lean months of the majority in their communities. Personal sufficiency in rice production is the *sine qua non* for accumulation of wealth and economic power for the individual, just as self-sufficiency in food production is the first step in any developing state. The man who grows enough rice and has a surplus is freed from the necessity of buying or working for his staple food, and can invest his time and surplus in the acquisition of still other resources.

Other techniques used by downriver farmers are similar to the techniques already described for shifting cultivators. The harvest's beginning is still marked by the ritual of "rice breaking" *(Matah Padi)* and harvesting is done by hand. Despite observation of Chinese methods of harvesting with a bushknife and threshing into a specially constructed box, downriver Iban have borrowed none of these innovations. The restraints of their theology are still sufficient to inhibit them from handling their life-stuff so roughly.

In most downriver communities, and in many upland regions as well, the Iban have access to gasoline-driven rice mills. These mills usually belong to the shopkeeper who mills the rice of other community members for a price. At Rumah Gaong, Enchul has operated such a mill for about ten years, and charges 35¢ for every picul (a British weight of approximately 133 pounds) of rice milled. The members of many communities have become quite dependent upon the convenience of mills, and several years ago Nyelang and his faction broke away from Imba and his relatives, maintaining that they were being exploited in Imba's shop and at his mill. Nyelang bought a mill, but it soon broke down, so that, to Imba's mild amusement—as he related the story to me—Nyelang and his faction had to come to Imba's mill, a distance of twenty minutes' walk.

Division of Labor and Returns

In wet rice farming, as in shifting cultivation, a major portion of the work falls to women. Where shifting cultivation is practiced, men help by felling trees and clearing the farms at the beginning of the year. Then they frequently absent themselves, especially during the period when the farms must be weeded. Men help carry the baskets of rice from the fields to the house at the end of the harvest and thresh the grain. But other tasks generally fall to women.

In wet rice cultivation, men may help clear the fields, using the pack-sprayers if this technique has been adopted. Men also may share in the hot and painful job of preparing the soil by chopping it with the *pito.* Where the use of drums is employed men usually roll the fields. Other work is done largely by women.

Table 6–2 presents the division of labor for wet rice farming at Rumah Nyala, together with the average number of workdays per acre in the various activities of farming. The workdays represent an average of the time actually spent by five families. The days for tasks such as building the farmhuts, weaving, winnowing, and storing are prorated according to acreage and the number of persons involved.

The average workday at the farm is about ten hours. Workers go to their farms before daylight and return at sundown. Calculating the average number of workdays by the length of the average working day, the Iban of Rumah Nyala invested about 700 hours per acre. The average yield per acre was 230 bushels of unhusked rice, or 138 bushels of husked rice, which sold in 1972 for 70¢ per bushel in Sibu. This represents an average return of $96.60 per acre, or an hourly wage of a little less than 14¢ for rice farming.

It should be noted that while this rate is well below the wages paid for some types of work, such as construction labor or employment with the government, it is above the amount that an

Table 6–2 Division of labor and workdays per acre

Type of Work	Men	Women	Work-days
Preparing the seedbed	X*	X	1
Clearing	X	X	7
Cultivating the soil	X	X	14
Building the farm hut	X		2
Transplanting	Y†	X	7
Weeding and fertilizing		X	14
Weaving mats, winnowing baskets, and seed baskets		X	2
Harvesting and transporting	X	X	17
Threshing	X	X	2
Drying	Y	X	2
Winnowing		X	1
Storage	Y	X	1
Total number workdays			70

* = major role
† = minor role

individual could make tapping rubber at the time of this study, when merchants in rural shops were paying 15¢ per sheet of unsmoked rubber. Work on one's own farm also was more rewarding than hiring out as a laborer to a fellow Iban for 70¢ per day.

The perception of returns from rice farming as low, however, has been important in the decision of many Iban who have left their rural communities to look for cash-paying jobs elsewhere, as we shall discuss later in this chapter.

We now shall examine the three major periods of economic change in the Rejang Valley and the effect that each has had on the Iban of the plains, and through their activities as cultural brokers to Iban in upriver areas.

RUBBER

Experiments in rubber planting were carried out in the lower Rejang from the first years of this century. Para rubber was introduced into the valley by a Chinese, whose lead was followed by his fellows when they realized that "rubber trees make money." The Iban took up rubber planting, and encouraged by the boom prices in 1910 set out their gardens along the lower Rejang, Leba'an, and Igan rivers.

Rubber production became a small-holder's industry, partially by the design of the second Rajah who wanted no interference from other Europeans in his state, and partially by necessity, owing to the limited capital available to local planters. By encouraging each family to plant its own rubber estate, the Rajah made ownership of real property and permanence of localized interests a new fact in Iban adaptation. In contrast to the mobility characteristic of shifting cultivators, owners of rubber gardens are more sedentary, living close to the trees they tap daily. As one Iban put it, "Our feet became stuck on the rubber."

Adaptation to rubber production was a shift in the value system and structure of Iban society. Whereas previously success in rice cultivation was essential for any male seeking recognition and upward mobility, rubber planting opened a new way to wealth and economic security. The conflict between traditional rice farming and rubber gardening was expressed in a widespread story to the effect that "rubber ate rice." In one version:

Aing, a farmer, put his rice out to dry on a mat and went off to his farm. When he returned the rice was gone. The next day the same thing happened. As there had been no wind on either day, Aing became suspicious. On the third day, he put his rice out to dry, but instead of going to his farm he sneaked back into his house and up to the loft where he could watch his rice. Slowly, slowly, before his eyes, the branches of a nearby rubber tree bent closer until the leaves, which are shaped like a dragon *(naga)* ate the rice.

As a result of this story and because of other pressures, an unknown number of Iban are alleged to have cut down their rubber trees, an act they were to regret later. Those men who refused to destroy their trees—to accede to tradition—reaped large profits during rubber booms. Under the tutelage of Chinese advisors, some invested their profits and emerged as wealthy men.

Another far-reaching effect of the Rajah's policy was the development of a statewide trading network to handle the exportation of rubber. This network involved Iban, Chinese, Malays, and other indigenes in the production of rubber with Chinese in the position of middlemen—until recently, when some Iban and Malay merchants have begun handling part of the rubber business. Until the growth of the timber industry, the exporting of rubber and the importing of foodstuffs, cloth, ironwares, outboard motors, and numerous other goods may be described as the backbone of the state's economy, necessary for the rise of traders among the major groups and to capital accumulation which has permitted investment in heavy equipment for the exploitation of Sarawak's major natural resource—timber.

Participation in the growth, tapping, and processing of rubber has made most Iban money wise and market conscious. The Iban are aware that the local market is part of world trade, and their activities reflect this awareness. At times when there has been a demand for rubber on the world market and prices have been high, Iban have tapped their trees and rushed the rubber sheets to market. When prices have dropped, tapping has declined to no more than is necessary for the purchase of sugar, salt, and coffee. In 1972 many Iban found it more profitable to hire out as laborers for eighty cents to one dollar a day than to tap their rubber trees.

The Iban have learned to play the market, to speculate and hold back quantities of rubber against a possible rise in prices. It is not at all uncommon to find several scores of rubber sheets hanging in village shops, or smaller amounts in the family apartments of longhouses, being held until prices rise or until the owners have enough sheets to make a trip to town. Many Iban cannot enjoy the luxury of such speculation, however, even on a small scale, and must sell soon after rolling the sheets regardless of prices.

Most rubber produced by Iban receives low prices because it contains impurities or—in some instances—is unsmoked. Some longhouse communities, though by no means a majority, have built smokehouses so that the profit for smoking their rubber sheets returns to them rather than to Chinese middlemen. The emergence of Iban traders at the village level has placed much more lower-level control of the rubber industry in the hands of Iban.

TIMBER

Sarawak has been described as a "timber-rich state," and what affluence the people of the state have enjoyed has derived largely from the timber industry. The value of Bornean timbers has long been recognized. As early as 1870, the famous rot-resistant and highly impervious ironwood was being exported from the middle Rejang to Hong Kong by Cantonese loggers. But the trade was spasmodic and there was no consistent demand for the timbers beyond the local market. Even up until the Second World War extraction of timber was difficult, because no mechanical equipment was used and the capital to purchase such equipment was unavailable.

The spectacular takeoff of the timber industry in Sarawak, which has dramatically affected the lives of many Iban as well as making more than one hundred Chinese millionaires, may be traced to several different factors. First *ramin (Gonstylus bancanus)*, formerly considered useless except for firewood by the indigenes, was found to be an excellent timber for moldings, furniture, and toys. *Ramin* is a yellow-white wood which was introduced into the United Kingdom market when there was a restriction on the import of softwoods into that country.

The *ramin* trade was centered in the Rejang delta, chiefly for two reasons: first, hydrographic surveys showed that it was possible for ocean-going freighters to cross the Rejang bar and anchor at the delta port of Tanjong Mani; second, the Rejang delta is the main forest area of Sarawak.

A second factor contributing to the growth of the timber industry was the accumulation of capital and a willingness to invest it in heavy equipment. This concerned Chinese exclusively. Like their compatriots in other parts of Southeast Asia, the Chinese of Sarawak were frugal and thrifty, bent on amassing enough savings to permit them to fulfill their "back-to-China" dream. The establishment of the People's Republic of China on the Asian mainland and the experiences of some overseas Chinese whose assets were seized upon their return to China dissuaded the wealthy senior Chinese of Sarawak from returning.

Realizing the rewards to be reaped in timber, Chinese families and friends formed companies, pooled their resources, and raised the capital necessary to purchase heavy equipment, build sawmills, and obtain cutting rights to forests.

The effects of the expansion of the timber industry have been felt by every community in the state. The government has benefited through revenue derived from royalties and permits paid by logging companies and sawmills for the right to cut timber, and from export duties. Most timber operations take place on state-controlled land, and permits must be obtained and royalties paid before felling can begin.

Owners and shareholders of timber companies have enjoyed generous returns from their investments. Profits realized from Rejang forests have financed new operations in other divisions of Sarawak, and in the Pontianak region of Kalimantan. Owners have consolidated their assets and assured their security by forming holding companies and branching into other businesses, principally banking and construction. Unbelievably large fortunes have been amassed by some Chinese; for example, the personal income of one of the most prominent Sibu businessmen was estimated at one million dollars per month.

The *nouveaux riches*—and they are in truth the "new rich,"

some of whom only twenty years ago lived in austere conditions in poorly equipped logging camps—engage in displays of wealth and power vis-à-vis others. These displays include the construction of large houses; the publicized performance of philanthropic acts and giving of gifts; the use of chauffeur-driven, air-conditioned cars, which in keeping with the "bigness" of the owners are outsized for many narrow streets; patronage of sporting competitions; and sending children abroad to private schools.

In a clear example of the "trickle-down effect," Iban and other indigenes have received monetary benefits from the timber industry. Iban communities have been paid concessions by timber companies for rights to fell "communal forests" (*Sarawak Gazette*, 31 August 1953). Gifts in the form of drinks and money have been made to area chiefs *(pengulu),* longhouse headmen *(tuai rumah),* and through them to the heads of families *(tuai bilik).* When an agreement on terms is reached by representatives of a timber company and community leaders, the *tuai rumah* involved present a request to the appropriate government ministry on behalf of the company—and at the expense of the company—for a logging permit.

In one instance two *tuai rumah* were given fifty dollars each and plane tickets to the state government in Kuching. Upon completion of negotiations, the company made a cash gift to the community, of which 60 percent went to the *pengulu,* 20 percent to the *tuai rumah,* and the balance was divided between other members of the community.

Recognizing the rewards to be gained, some Iban have shown a marked proclivity for claim-jumping. For example, two Iban from the Igan River area attempted to establish rights to negotiate with a company for a tract of land up the Naman River, some two hours travel from their home. They were outdone by an Iban from another community who duped the company representatives and got the cash gift—and later a jail term—for selling rights to the forest to which he had no legal rights.

A further effect of the timber industry has been the employment of Iban and other indigenes in sawmills and logging operations. Prior to a slight decline in mid-1971, employers in these operations provided work for an estimated 20,000 men and were the largest employers of industrial labor in Sarawak. In a survey of 37 longhouses in the Sibu District, every house had one or more persons who has worked or is working in some aspect of timber. More than 1,000 Iban were employed in the Sibu Section of the Forest Department. Others work as far away as Miri, Bintulu, Tawau (Sabah), and Kalimantan. Recruitment is often done by an Iban agent who enlists relatives and friends, and who receives a commission for his recruiting activities.

In some cases Iban workers commute daily from nearby long-houses, for example from the large community at Bawang Assan to Kong Thai Sawmill just above the division of the Rejang and Leba'an rivers. In other instances, Iban live in camps for several weeks. In still other situations, Iban who are recruited for jobs in the Fifth Division, Sabah, or Indonesia may remain away for from two to ten years.

It is interesting to note that Iban are second to Melanau among the indigenous timber workers. The reason given by Chinese employers is that even rather acculturated Iban are prone to quit suddenly if they have a bad dream or hear an omen bird, unlike the Melanau who are not affected by such cultural inhibitions. (One wonders how often dreams and inauspicious birds "appear" as a way out of an undesirable situation.)

One final effect of the timber industry and the amount of cash made available to Iban has been an increased sensitization to the buying power and desire for cash. Just as we refer—albeit incorrectly—to housewives as "working" or "not working" according to whether they are earning wages, so also the Iban have adopted the same principle to define "work/non-work." On several occasions I heard references to men who were said to be "not working" *(enda' bekereja),* and I knew that the men under discussion were farming. But when I raised a question about the men and what they were doing, the discussants insisted that only wage earning can be properly described as "work."

The desire for cash—not only its acquisition but also its retention—has led to saving, a decidedly nontraditional Iban practice. Acquisition customarily has been accompanied by distribution, whether in simple gifts of game, fish, or other food-stuffs, or in more elaborate festivals. Such distribution was important in the ecology of the Iban in that it militated against undue or unequal want. It was important in the sociology of the

Iban, most of whom subscribed to a practice of "share and share alike." The desire to retain money is an expression of acculturation and differentiation that the Iban are experiencing. Many see in the values of other groups, particularly Chinese and Europeans, styles of life that appear attractive. They resist and resent the demands of their peers and the leveling process by which the Iban have maintained an egalitarian ethic. They are determined that they are going to be less like Iban of the past and more like other groups of the present.

It is interesting and important to note that retention and emulation are expressed concretely among the Iban who live in or near urban centers. An increasing number of Iban are opening savings accounts in banks. For example, a leading bank of Sibu handles an estimated 3,000 savings accounts for Iban. Asked why he put his money in a savings account, one Iban replied, "It's the only way I can keep my relatives and friends from knowing what I have, and can keep it for myself."

PEPPER

Next to rubber, pepper is Sarawak's most valuable agricultural export. During the postwar era, Sarawak has ranked with Indonesia and India as one of the three leading producers. Although there is a long history of pepper planting in parts of Sarawak, the foundations of the modern industry were laid by the second Rajah who offered free passage and free land to Chinese farmers.

In the Sibu District, Chinese immigrants planted pepper in the early 1900s, but booming rubber prices together with severe limitations of well-drained soils available to them, resulted in the eclipse of pepper by rubber among the Chinese. The expansion of Foochow and Cantonese settlements into Binatang and Sarikei was accompanied by the planting of hundreds of pepper gardens.

Although the pepper industry remains largely a Chinese preserve, many Iban have realized that pepper is a valuable supplement to rubber as a source of cash, and where soils are suitable have planted pepper gardens. A major problem confronting Iban planters is a lack of capital to plant the vines in large numbers. In most cases, the Iban farmer plants between

150 and 350 vines. In addition to vines, he must purchase iron-wood posts on which the vines climb, and fertilizers. The Agriculture Department helps with herbicides and pesticides.

The Iban also lacks the experience that the Chinese has gained over the past seventy years, and the Iban's plants suffer accordingly. His inexperience manifests itself as he plants in poorly drained soil, does not practice balanced fertilization, or sprays his plants with concentrations of pesticides that are too strong, causing the leaves to fall off. Consequently, the Iban planter realizes a yield of between five to seven pounds per vine, whereas the Chinese averages between eleven to thirteen pounds per vine.

Vines begin bearing between three and four years after planting. The berries are picked between May and August each year. After they are picked, the berries are taken to the long-house (in the case of Iban) where they are sorted and cleaned of stems and twigs by all members of the family on the covered verandah. After being thoroughly cleaned, the pepper is dried on the open porch, being turned occasionally with a wood-bladed spreader. When the pepper is dry it is transferred to gunnysacks which, when full, weight about 190 pounds. On an average, an Iban planter can receive up to $300 from 250 vines.

DIVERSIFICATION OF ADAPTIVE STRATEGIES

The greatest changes that have occurred among the Iban who have moved to the lower and middle Rejang are (1) adoption of wet-rice, permanent field cultivation and the appropriate techniques, and (2) a diversification of economic activities. Although certain techniques, such as gathering, fishing, and hunting, still are practiced, generally they are of less importance in the food quest of the Iban. Much greater attention is paid to the fields, an average of 700 work-hours per acre of wet rice in contrast to an average of 425 work-hours per acre of dry rice. And the most important supplementary activities are those that yield cash returns.

Rumah Nyala, Sungai Aup, is one of the most acculturated Iban communities. The first units of the new longhouse were constructed by Malay carpenters whose skill and materials stand in stark contrast to non-professionally built units. The community has a water pump connecting the house to the Aup River, some 400 yards away. Members have wired their houses, which are lit by a community-sponsored generator.

Among the economically active members of Rumah Nyala, it is instructive to note that there are more wage earners than there are persons whose principal activity is farming. Forty-two members, predominantly women, farm, tap rubber, collect foodstuffs, and work at other traditional activities. Fifty-seven members, predominantly men, work in Sibu, which is about one-half hour's bicycle ride from the community, as well as in other parts of Sarawak. Members of the latter group are employed as laborers, teachers, gardeners, custodians, movie projectionists, medical workers, and in various branches of the military.

Every family unit in Rumah Nyala with the exception of Kudi's has at least one wage earner, and one unit has five. (Kudi is a cripple who lives alone and is supported by his brother, the Pengarah [second to paramount chief or *Temenggong*] Chundi.) We shall consider later the implications of such changes in the adaptive strategies of the Iban for their social organization; suffice it here to note that for the most part diversification has meant a broadening of economic bases and the development of mutually supportive relations between farmers and wage earners. For example, Ganai of Rumah Nyala farms and works in Sibu as a gardener. His daughter married an Iban police inspector, who helps Ganai with money, sugar, and coffee each month and receives in return rice and whatever jungle foods Ganai's wife, Nunsong, collects. "As long as we have our farm and he his job," said Ganai, "neither of us will go hungry."

Enchul of Rumah Gaong, Sungai Sengan, is illustrative of downriver Iban who maintain their ethnic identity while participating more actively and frequently in their modernizing society. Enchul was born in the old house of Rumah Imba, Salim, in about 1932. He had four brothers, one of whom was an adopted Chinese. Enchul's father died when Enchul was fourteen. All of the brothers moved out of their family unit when they married, except the adopted Chinese who still lives with and cares for Enchul's elderly mother.

Following his father's death, Enchul went to school at Bawan for about six months. He was older than the other students and embarrassed to be studying with them, but he was more determined to learn to read and write, skills that he acquired in about six months. While in school he was especially keen on arithmetic—unusual for most Iban—and upon his return home a local Chinese shopkeeper taught him how to keep accounts and to do simple figuring. He also gave Enchul advice on how to buy and sell goods for a profit.

Like most young Iban men, Enchul went traveling to see more of the country and to learn as much as possible. He worked at Miri for three months, painting pipes used by Shell Oil for pumping gas to ships anchored offshore. He moved on to Baram where he worked for five months, tapping rubber on the edge of the jungle. After he had saved enough money for the trip home and to begin trading, he returned to Salim.

After his return to Salim, his mother arranged for him to marry his third cousin who lived in Sengan. In 1952 Enchul was married, and because his wife was an only child, the adopted daughter of her parents, he went to live with her family. Before going on his trip Enchul had saved $460, and he had accumulated another $135 during his travels. He had tried to save the money on the advice of the Chinese shopkeeper who had told him how much money he would need to begin trading. Enchul's father-in-law already had obtained a license to trade in the Sengan area, but had not opened a shop because he knew that he could not carry it on alone and he did not trust any of his neighbors. Therefore, when Enchul married, his father-in-law agreed for him to open a shop at the edge of their front porch.

Enchul started his shop by purchasing essential items—matches, kerosene, sugar, salt, and some canned goods—which he sold to members of the community. In return he bought rubber and pepper from them. The first years were filled with hard work as he tried to establish his business. Supplies had to be bought in Sibu, and the goods he purchased from community members had to be taken to market. He paddled an eighteen-foot dugout down the twisting, log-choked Sengan stream to the mouth of the Menyan where he loaded his cargo of rubber and pepper onto a Chinese motor launch going to Sibu. (When the water is high the trip from the mouth of the Menyan to Enchul's house takes about one hour. In 1958 when I first met Enchul, a four-week dry spell had so shrunk the Sengan, however, that my first trip to his house took almost ten hours.) The trip from Rumah Gaong to Sibu took Enchul two days. He spent one day in Sibu doing business, and returned to Sengan, arriving home late on the fifth day. As he prospered, he hired two helpers—a prowsman to guide the bow of the dugout around the narrow bends and past submerged logs, and a bailer. After three years he had saved enough to buy a small five and one-half horsepower outboard motor.

In contrast to numerous ventures by Iban into shopkeeping, Enchul has been unusually successful. There are two principal reasons for his success. First, he has been shrewd enough to extend credit, yet forceful enough to collect his debts. Many Iban-operated shops have been closed because the owners either refused to extend credit, thereby alienating their customers, or have overextended credit, bankrupting themselves. On first meeting Enchul gives the impression of being a silly, happy-go-lucky clod. The disarming effect of this impression is, however, quite purposeful, for the more familiar one becomes with Enchul, the more one is impressed with how capable he is at making out for himself simply by getting along with other people.

The second reason for Enchul's success is his ability to combine the traditional value of self-sufficiency with the more modern—Chinese—value of thrift. Accounting for his rise as a trader, Enchul attributed it directly to his family's productive farming. In his own words:

I have never had a bad year of farming. My family has never known want. Because I have not had to buy rice, and often had some to sell, I have been able to save and to invest my money. Year by year I have been able to build up my savings. Also, I am thrifty and not wasteful —I don't play around with other women, because I figure I am already married.

Unlike 90 percent of the members of his community, Enchul has a surplus of rice every year. In his opinion, success in farming is mostly a matter of careful timing and hard work:

Only one-tenth of the people in our house have enough rice because the others don't know how to farm. Some plant too early, others too late. Some clear their fields but don't weed them, some weed but don't harvest carefully. It's not so much a matter of luck or land. We farm the same kind of land as those who don't get rice, and we have a surplus every year. It depends on hard work (*tulang*, "bone"), not land. Those who are short of rice aren't unlucky, but either don't know how to farm or don't do what they know.

Because of their outstanding success in farming, Enchul's family often loans rice to other families in exchange for labor at a rate of five and one-third pounds of rice, or 70¢, for one day's work.

Unlike many Iban who have sold their land near the roads to realize quick gains from Chinese, Enchul has bought all the land he can afford. Together with Embuas, the son of Tuai Rumah Imba, he has purchased all of the land two lots deep on both sides of the Durin Road from Mile 5½ to Mile 8½.

By Enchul's assessment:

Most Iban don't know how to handle the changes that are taking place. An Iban sells his land and hands the money right back to the Chinese from whom he buys things. I tell the people in my house that the Chinese give thanks to Tua Peh Kong (God of the Earth) for us Iban who are giving them our land and our money, too.

In 1960 Enchul bought a rice mill, explaining that he thought it too much trouble for women from his house to have to pound rice or to have to take it an hour's trip to the nearest mill. After purchasing the mill, Enchul had money left and bought two tracts of land west of the longhouse for $135. He built a cattle shed and bought fourteen head of cattle, a hearty type that could live on the scrub and grass found on the land. Recently he obtained three species of grass and has started a small nursery from which he hopes to supplement his cattle's diet.

When plans for opening a road were announced by the government, Enchul immediately began to find a way to buy a car and to learn to drive. In 1966, after the government road had been cut through the forest some three miles from Rumah Gaong, he bought an Austin van for $3,285.

I studied how to drive—really studied—because we Iban didn't know how to drive. I didn't hire a teacher, as most learners do, but studied with Chinese [with] whom I was familiar. Because they had never seen an Iban drive a car for profit, the Chinese didn't charge me, figuring that I was just going to play around with my car.

After he thought that he knew enough, Enchul went to Sibu and made arrangements to take a test for his license. He and three Iban companions met a Chinese who assured them that for $35 each he could arrange for them to get their licenses without having to take the examination. The Chinese took their money, skipped to Brunei, and when the four Iban were told that they could not get their licenses without an examination, they realized that they had been swindled. Enchul subsequently passed his test for a taxi driver's license, and he now operates his own taxi from his house to Sibu. His passengers pay his travel expenses, and he is able to use the trips he makes twice each day for transporting goods to and from the market.

In some respects Enchul is typical of the downriver Iban, and in others he is atypical. He shows the capacity for pioneering and adventure that have marked the Iban male, yet he also has accommodated to values that are more often associated with the Chinese. He continues to define his achievements in terms of rice farming, yet he has resisted pressures to distribute his surpluses in feasts. He maintains a concern for his community members, providing rice in exchange for labor and the services of his mill at a price, and exults in being able to retain his profits and having prospered at the expense of his peers.

Enchul is representative of those downriver Iban who have had more intimate contact with alien groups than have most members of his community, and certainly more familiarity than most upriver Iban. Like others who maintain their residence in or have at least enjoyed frequent contacts with their longhouse communities, Enchul acts as a cultural broker, interpreting the values of alien societies and thus contributing to a growth of the cognized environment to which the Iban are adapting.

Chapter 7

SIBU, THE PORT TOWN: ITS GROWTH AND IMPORTANCE

One of the landmarks that has assumed increasing importance in the lives of the Iban, both upriver and downriver, has been the port town and administrative center. Sibu and other such towns in Sarawak grew around forts established during the Brooke Raj, and like most urban centers in Southeast Asia they function chiefly as *entrepôts* through which pass local produce and imported goods. Understandably, these towns have developed as administrative centers where successive governments —Brooke, British, and Malaysian—have located their offices and focused their powers, which they have continuously extended over the lives of their citizens.

Sibu may be described quite legitimately as a town that grew because of the Iban. Although the "Great Tradition–Little Tradition" model, which described the direction of influence as moving from superordinate to subordinate group, has been refuted by numerous ethnographic studies, still one more will do no harm and may contribute to the realization that influence moves in both directions in contact situations. This certainly was the case in Sarawak during the nineteenth century when the Brookes, determined to suppress headhunting and inhibit Iban migrations, dotted the map at strategic points with forts.

Just as Fort Brooke on Sibu Island was founded because of the Iban, so too was much of the trade conducted near the fort in the last quarter of the nineteenth century dependent upon produce supplied by Iban and other indigenes. Munan, whom we considered earlier, was a leading businessman and rubber planter. He and other Iban were "landowners" in what is now Sibu suburbia.

During this century, however, the power of the once independent Iban has declined as Sibu has become the locus of authority. Power has shifted from the family and longhouse community to the government, which controls natural resources, validates landholdings, enforces laws, issues radio and bicycle licenses, collects taxes, and functions as patron through the services it provides.

DEVELOPMENT OF ADMINISTRATIVE FUNCTIONS

A Center for Pacification

The first purpose of the construction of Fort Brooke in 1862 was pacification of the area under its jurisdiction so that economic development could take place. Although the acquisition of the Rejang Valley was accomplished by the Brookes in the treaties of 1853 and 1861, the terms of the treaties had to be backed by force of arms. Half a century after the first treaty was signed, the Rejang was described in the *Sarawak Gazette* as being still "in an unsettled state" (June 4, 1904).

Fort Brooke became the central base of operations from which the Rajah's decrees were distributed, fines meted out to offenders and, when necessary, parties dispatched to enforce government policies or to carry out punitive raids. Iban leaders who mounted opposition to the Brooke government were brought to Sibu either for punishment or temporary incarceration.

We have described the forced settlements of Munan and his followers who were required to move from the Krian to Sibu, and of Lintong who had to leave the Julau to move under the fort's surveillance. Similarly, the dissident Poi Iban were made to settle in the Igan where they could be kept under control.

The original staff of the fort was small, numbering less than fifty men. The staff comprised of Englishmen and Sepoys was necessarily an alien one in the beginning. The strength of the

Brooke administration did not derive, however, from the staff but rather from the adept manipulation of various Iban factions against one another by the Brooke Rajahs, particularly Charles, the second Rajah. By the forging of alliances with some Iban factions against others, the Brookes were able to exert their authority over even the most incorrigible leaders who were forced to settle under the shadow of the symbol of Brooke rule —the fort.

The measure of Brooke's success in usurping traditional authority is evident in the fact that by the beginning of this century, Iban were members of the Sarawak Constabulary. By joining this organization Iban were offered a legitimate means to adventure and violence which otherwise were denied them. The entrance of Iban into the constabulary was a tacit admission of the supremacy of the Brooke administration, whose laws Iban now served to enforce. That the Iban recognize this transfer of authority, and a functional equivalence between the traditional role of headhunter and the contemporary role of policeman or ranger, was dramatically shown in a "Feast of the Dead Spirits" *(Gawai Antu)* which I observed at Rumah Bebuling, Spaoh, in Sarawak's Second Division in 1970. Along with two notable former headhunters, two rangers who had killed terrorists were permitted to drink the sacred rice wine *(ai' garong)* which previously could be drunk only by men who had taken a human head.

Courts

The growth of the court system may be attributed at least in part to the Iban's proclivity for litigation and preference of an outsider as arbiter. As the *Sarawak Gazette* and other historical documents show, by the last decade of the nineteenth century the Iban had recognized the courts as a new arena in which to contest their rights to property. Use of and appeal to the courts has by no means diminished, and each day scores of Iban are in town because of cases to be heard by the District Officer or Magistrate.

The Iban traditionally expect that favoritism will be shown by the native Iban arbiter who follows customary law, which is personal and based upon the arbiter's familiarity with the litigants. Thus the arbiter is very much subject to pressure from each litigant and his faction which often directs the outcome of the verdict. In contrast, the Iban feel that the government officer follows formal law, which is less personal and ideally requires that the arbiter be unacquainted with the litigants so that he may apply the law impartially on the merits of the case.

While admittedly domestic disputes within a longhouse must be heard by the head of the house, and interhouse cases must be tried by the *Pengulu*, the Iban are nonetheless aware that grievances over the decisions rendered by these officials may be appealed—often, pointlessly—to the District Office. The purpose of such appeals is manifold, and includes efforts to gain redress against unjust judgments, attempts to subvert the authority of headmen and *Pengulu*, and hope for support for and alliance with a more powerful authority.

In short, litigations arising from the divisions that existed and continue to exist in Iban society weakened the internal political and decision-making processes by ascribing ultimate control to external authorities. While appeal to government courts may indeed have assured the Iban of a better chance for an impartial judgment, it also strengthened the government's control of the Iban.

Political Integration

A further development which has enlarged the importance of towns such as Sibu on the cognitive maps of the Iban was the creation of an hierarchical structure of authority into which the Iban were integrated. Whereas the Iban had produced no surplus, precluding the rise of permanent leaders, they acknowledged the leadership of individuals only on an ad hoc basis. The shaman *(manang)* performed rites of curing. The augur *(tuai burong)* divined the outcome of events of moment. And the various war leaders (*tuai kayau*, "head of a raiding party," *tau' serang*, "brave," and *raja berani*, "wealthy brave") rose to prominence on the occasion of raids.

The second Rajah established a network of power ties with himself at the vortex, a system which was in stark contrast to the impermanence of leadership among the egalitarian Iban. The Rajah's efforts were in keeping with the political philosophy of his time, and he attempted to avoid disruption of Iban life by establishment of "indirect rule." The effect, however, was to bring into being a form of political organization with government support in which appointed Iban leaders enjoyed more authority and security than they ever had known under the traditional system.

At the lowest level, Iban longhouse communities were required to select headmen *(tuai rumah)* who adjudicated problems and land disputes internal to the community. At a higher level were the *Pengulu* (alternately, *Penghulu*), a position appropriated by the Rajah from Malay political organization and used among the Iban at the first investiture in Sibu in 1883 (cf. *Sarawak Gazette,* September 1, 1883). At the third level was a diverse native service with a corps of Native Officers, above them the Divisional Residents, and at the apex the Rajah.

The creation of the status of *Pengulu* had far-reaching implications in the loosely structured Iban political organization. The *Pengulu* were to supervise collection of an annual family tax and to receive a commission of 10 percent on all taxes collected. The *Pengulu* were empowered to judge interhouse disputes, such as quarrels over land boundaries, adultery, or cases which the *tuai rumah* could not resolve. In the Rejang, the *Pengulu* were allowed to levy fines on which they received a commission of 10 percent. In the mid-1920s, under the third Rajah, the *Pengulu* began to receive salaries in lieu of commissions on taxes and fines.

The *Pengulu* were expected to visit each of the communities in their jurisdiction at least once a year to hear cases and to keep in touch with local situations, and to apprise the residents of longhouse communities of government policies and activities which affected them. In 1939 the "Counselor's House" *(Rumah Kunsil),* known from 1950 to 1970 as the Iban Guest House *(Rumah Temuai Iban),* was built beside the stream flowing past Sibu Island and Queensway Road. This house had seven rooms, one for each of the seven *Pengulu* of the Sibu District, in which they could stay while in Sibu. There also was a central room where cases could be heard, one of the requirements being that a government counsel be present to record the details of the cases.

The building of the "Counselor's House" was the first step in a development of the increasing townward orientation of the Iban of the Sibu District. Implicit in the house's construction

was the Brooke administration's desire to regulate and central-
ize the activities of the *Pengulu.* This desire is understandable,
given the abuse of the office by some *Pengulu.* Nevertheless,
the message conveyed through the *Pengulu's* court set up in
the *Rumah Kunsil* was that their constituents were to come to
them rather than vice versa. The climax of this development
has taken place during the past decade during which there has
been a virtual cessation of the *Pengulu's* visits to longhouses. As
a result, Iban having cases to be tried must come to Sibu where
all of the *Pengulu,* with the exception of Pengulu Gelau of the
lower Igan, spend much of their time. Two of the district's
Pengulu have permanent residence in the town; two come
several days each week; a fifth stays in town for weeks at a time;
and the sixth has left the area of his jurisdiction (Menyan) and
during the past three years has farmed on Kerto Island opposite
the town.

The District Office

Another of the administrative branches by which the
Iban have become sensitized to the town and its importance in
their lives is the District Office. The most important positions
in the office as far as the Iban are concerned are (1) the District
Officer, who in Sibu is the administrative head of the district,
and (2) the Sarawak Administrative Officer. The latter handles
a multitude of requests, ranging from property matters to applications for travel permits which the Iban must obtain if they
intend to seek work in another political division. The District
Officer is an advisor to the Urban and Rural Councils, and all
policy matters of both councils must be channeled through him
for his information, though not necessarily for his approval. The
District Officer also is the Probate Officer, handling all estates
of money or land that must be probated.

All deeds to property must be registered in the District
Office. The surveying of land, including Iban holdings, has
served to orient the Iban to the office as the authority in land
matters. Land disputes that are not settled to the satisfaction of
all parties by the longhouse headman or *Pengulu* may be appealed to the District Officer.

From 1934 to the present, records of all Iban cases heard by
a *Pengulu* have been entered in the "Dayak Report." Each

Pengulu is required to submit an account of his travels and an appraisal of conditions existing in each longhouse visited during his tours, which theoretically are made twice each year and on special occasions. The District Office is custodian of the "*Pengulu* Tin System," a set of boxes containing a directory of all longhouses and censuses of each. The materials in the boxes are a valuable source of information about the residence patterns of Iban, longitudinal profiles of families, and the evolution of longhouse communities.

All guns owned by Iban must be licensed in the District Office. (Records in the storage area beneath the stairs behind the District Office present an interesting pattern in the introduction of and demand for guns, principally shotguns, for both utilitarian and prestige purposes.) Because all ammunition must be bought from the District Office, fresh cartridges being sold only upon submission of discharged casings, the government has been able to maintain control of the persons who may obtain ammunition and, in effect, use guns.

District Councils

In January 1952, the Sibu Urban District Council and the Sibu Rural District Council were formed. The latter, a multiracial organization with power over rural areas, was established to replace the Sea Dayak (Iban) Local Authority. The rural council is composed of members elected from twenty-two wards; eight of the members are Iban.

Each family head has at least an annual contact with the council when he pays his house tax, which is based on the rentable value of property. In the case of the Iban, each family unit *(bilik)* is taxed an amount of $1.20 to $1.40 depending upon the age of the longhouse. In addition, Iban must pay a 35¢ tax for each shotgun, $3.35 for a radio license, 35¢ per acre of farmland, and $1.00 per acre of rubber garden. The council also is the license-issuing authority for all rural shops, an increasing number of which are operated by Iban traders.

Within the last decade or so, services sponsored by the Rural District Council have been expanded and much sought for by Iban from almost every community. The Iban have always had a keen appetite for profit and maximizing their opportunities. As a result of observing the rewards that schooling has brought to those who were able to get positions as teachers and as government and company clerks, many community leaders have requested that a school be placed "at the foot of the (longhouse) ladder" *(di kaki tangga')*, an expression used by Alli Majang, an officer in the Education Department, and others to describe the Iban's desire for the proliferation of schools.

In addition to responsibility for primary school education, the Council provides maternity and child care in the district, employing and training midwives who either reside near or travel to rural communities. The education provided by these midwives in both antenatal and postnatal care of mothers and infants has resulted in a significant decrease in mortality rates related to maternity cases.

Codification of Customary Law

The Brookes' respect for local customary law and their strong determination to bring these laws into line with Western codes resulted in a number of meetings of the Rajahs' representatives with Iban knowledgeable in their laws. One of the most important of these meetings was held in 1932 when every *Pengulu* except one in the Rejang Valley met in Sibu with the Tuan Muda ("Young Master") Bertram Brooke and other government officials. Participants in the meeting began by listing all controversial customs and penalties, and debate was held on each aspect of traditional law about which there was disagreement. After a consensus had been reached, the leaders returned to consult with their constituents, and following another meeting and final discussion the Iban law for the Third Division was drafted.

Although the Rajah's and the Colonial Government's efforts to codify Iban customary law led to publication of the *Tusun Tunggu,* a list of offenses with appropriate fines, it is impossible to comprehend customary law in a neatly arranged code. As one anonymous student of customary law has noted:

The *adat* (law) of Sarawak is neither simple nor straigtforward and is not to be traced to any one source . . . *Adat* has remained *adat* in its pure form, a rule of tradition to be found only in the mind of society (*Sarawak Gazette,* May 31, 1952).

One incident may illustrate the complexity of customary law. I once found a young child critically ill with diphtheria in a longhouse above Kanowit, and the parents asked if I would take them and the child to a clinic at Kanowit. We had traveled about twenty minutes when the mother began to cry the distinctive wail when one has died. We returned to the jetty but were prevented from taking the body back into the house we had left about forty-five minutes earlier. We waited with the child's body in a clearing before the house for two hours while the *tuai rumah* and family heads discussed the size of a sacrifice necessary to propitiate any spirits which might have followed us. Finally it was agreed that one pig and three chickens would be killed, after which sacrifice we were permitted to enter the house.

Attempts to codify Iban law were consonant with the philosophy of indirect rule to which the Brookes gave intellectual assent. It permitted them to select and support those features of customary law that were congenial with their purpose and to make them normative through implementation by government-appointed leaders.

The difficulty of integrating customary and formal law is exemplified further in the land disputes which broke out between Chinese and Iban in the first year of Chinese immigration. These disputes reached a climax in the "Binatang Disputes of 1925."

The problems that arose were in part technical, in part cultural, and basically related to the two groups' use and attitudes toward land. The Chinese, coming from the overpopulated southeastern provinces of China, saw the largely unsettled areas of the Rejang Valley as land free for occupation and cultivation. The land which the Iban had cleared of virgin jungle and which was covered with secondary growth looked especially inviting. What the Chinese did not understand, and what the Rajahs surprisingly would not comprehend, was the Iban attitude toward the land. The conflict basically was one between settlers whose farming techniques included the complete clearing and fertilization of land for permanent occupation and continuous cultivation, and shifting cultivators, whose techniques included clearing land sufficiently to place rice amidst the stumps for one or two years, then moving on, but claiming usufruct rights in perpetuity and assuming responsibilities to the spirits of those who had invested their energies and lives in the land.

In the second Rajah's attempt to resolve Chinese-Iban disputes and to establish land laws, he set aside land on both sides of the Rejang for a distance of twelve miles below Sibu for Chinese settlers, requiring Iban and other non-Chinese to move immediately from the area. Despite his efforts—or more correctly, because of his efforts—encroachments of Chinese onto Iban land continued, and the land laws promulgated during his reign and that of his successor have never entirely supplanted traditional Iban attitudes toward land.

Commenting on the problem of land laws in Sarawak, Edmund Leach observed:

In my experience the administrator discussing land rights with a peasant is usually talking at cross purposes; for the former, "my land" implies a personal individual form of tenure; for the latter it may involve a host of obligations toward abstrusely connected relatives not to mention their ancestral spirits (*Sarawak Gazette*, August 1, 1947).

While the laws instituted by the Rajahs did not supplant the more traditional laws, they nevertheless have had far-reaching effects in the lives of the Iban. To note but one example, the establishment of the Land and Survey Department as an external authority to validate land tenure radically changed the social organization of the Iban. The practice of preserving lengthy genealogies (cf. Salisbury, 1956), up to thirty generations in depth, as a means of establishing right to cultivate land is rapidly disappearing among Iban of the Sibu District. Authority now is vested in the title. Whereas individual ownership of land was an anomaly in traditional Iban society, Nuya of Rumah Nyala, Aup, privately purchased several tracts of land in upriver Mukah where her husband taught school and she was in charge of boarding facilities.

Protection of Resources

The establishment of the Forest Department in Sibu during the year 1919 provided another thread binding the Iban of the Rejang to the town. The department was established to constitute and administer various categories of forests.

The flourishing of the timber industry in the late 1940s and 1950s required overall supervision to guard against indiscriminate felling of forests. Of concern to the Iban were the longhouse communal forests which were important to them for building materials for their houses, for firewood, and for the products which they consume and sell. The rapidly expanding timber operations caused many Iban to fear that the forests and their products might be irretrievably lost. As a result, petitions were made by the headmen of many longhouses, and where possible and reasonable the Forest Department established communal forests which could not be cut by timber companies, but instead were the preserves of the respective communities. Unfortunately, in some cases the headmen did not make petitions until all the forest near their longhouses had been allocated to other houses, or they made applications for forests some distance away, claiming customary rights they were unable to substantiate. Ironically, in the timber-rich state of Sarawak there are some longhouse communities without rights to any forests, and others that by sale of their lands are totally impoverished of natural resources.

The constitution of some forests as Native Forest Reserves has permitted the removal of timber by logging companies with the profits going to the Iban, as was discussed previously. With the booming timber prices and the desire for cash coupled with their strategic control over the Native Forest Reserves, some Iban have been able to use their ethnic membership and political titles to advantage. For example, those *Pengulu* and headmen who have been able to acquire rights to forests sought by timber operators have been able to convert these political advantages into personal economic benefits.

PERMITS AND PROBATE

Additional evidence of the growing importance of the town in the lives of Iban is the number of estates that are brought to the Sibu District Office for probate. Although, as one informant stated, this is a relatively new phenomenon, and not many Iban are aware of probate procedures, the available figures indicate that Iban estates accounted for almost one-third of those probated in Sibu. For example, in 1952, the first year for which figures are available, Iban estates numbered 37 of a total of 105 probated.

The inclination of Iban to have their estates probated in the District Office is due to several factors. First is the Iban principle of partible inheritance. With the exception of smoked heads, all other objects in a family may be divided among their heirs. Division is usually made by the heirs themselves; if they fail to agree on the division, the headman may be asked to determine the share of each heir.

Second, as we have discussed, as the Iban moved into the lower and middle Rejang, they planted rubber gardens and began the cultivation of swamp rice. Instead of cultivating and moving on, as had been their practice, they invested time, energy, and money in the development of their lands. With Chinese immigrations reaching flood proporations by the mid-1920s, it became expedient if not imperative for Iban to acquire Occupation Tickets to guarantee their rights to farmlands and rubber gardens. Without an Occupation Ticket an Iban faced possible litigation over and removal from land to which he claimed usufruct rights, but to which a Chinese had been granted a temporary title. For example, in 1925, when 4,000 Chinese immigrants arrived in Sibu, a total of 3,100 temporary titles or Occupation Tickets were issued for "newly opened land," much of which was still claimed by Iban who had farmed it within the past decade.

Because Iban estates that are probated are composed of real property, such as farmlands or rubber gardens, Iban are becoming more aware of the desirability of having a clear title or permit to land. When a permit to real property is inherited by an individual, he has the name on the permit changed from that of the deceased to his own in the District Office and pays the transfer fee. When several persons inherit the same land that is under permit, it is sometimes necessary for new permits to be issued according to the division of the property among the heirs who share payment of the probate charge.

In summary, the growth of administrative functions in Sibu has been accompanied by an extension of influence and control over the Iban. During the past century there has been a shift in the locus of power over natural resources, political offices, interhouse relations, personal responsibilities, the interpretation of law, and the validation of personal rights from the longhouse, which as we shall discuss later was the Iban's "center of the universe," to the town, which is the new center of "the world."

SIBU AS A TRADING CENTER

Sibu is a market town that has been built out of and continues to be dependent upon the surrounding forests. Lacking any significant industrialization, the town and most of its 70,000 residents are dependent upon the trading of exports and imports.

The town began as a cluster of Chinese shops built around Fort Brooke. By 1880, or eighteen years after establishment of the fort, Hokkien traders had built two rows of forty shophouses each along what now is Channel Road. By 1903 the first Foochow-owned shophouses were built on the same road.

Well into the first decade of this century trade was light and irregular. The principal items for export were the various jungle products collected on a casual basis according to the whims of the indigenous collectors who were guided by numerous symbols. The reading of a poorly lined pig's liver, a bad dream, the cry of an omen bird, or a bird's flight from the left rather than the right could result in a collecting trip being called off. Thus indigenes sometimes appeared laden with goods for exchange, but more often they did not.

The distance of Sibu from the sea and the difficulty of navigating the Rejang with its treacherous sandbars prevented many ocean-going vessels from calling at the town. Because the Rejang below Sarikei could be navigated only on a rising tide, the visits of ships in and out of Sibu were very irregular.

The introduction of rubber overcame the problem of a regularly available exportable product. Rubber, and to a lesser extent pepper, provided products of more predictable and dependable character than the sometimes available, casually gathered jungle products.

The problem of shipping was a persistent one. At the point of division of the Rejang and the Leba'an both banks are lined by sandbars on which ships have gone aground, occasionally being stranded for two to three days until the confluence of higher waters from upriver and the incoming tide allowed them to float. Sharp bends and shallows below that division often required that ships delay their sailing until they could catch the tide, and even then captains had to proceed with utmost caution.

The problem was solved in 1961 with the discovery of a deep-water passage into the Rejang River through the Paloh River. The passage permitted larger ocean-going vessels up to 5,000 tons to call at Sibu, and made the town the thriving port that it has become.

By 1920 the market area of Sibu had expanded to handle the increased volume of business. The increased trade provided employment for Chinese who either were landless or not inclined to farming. Despite the growth of trade, the building of shophouses, and the involvement of more people in trade, unemployment problems continued. When rubber prices were high, owners of rubber gardens took on workers to help tap the trees. But when the prices fell, the tappers were released in hundreds and were unable to find work. The government took on as many men as possible and set them to road-building and clearance of new agricultural sites.

The immediate importance of this development was that it established a pattern which still is held to and practiced by not only Chinese but also Iban and other indigenes. As a result, if rice crops fail and the price of rubber falls, men and women come into the town to seek temporary day-labor, such as unloading charcoal from lighters, or more permanent work with distilleries or construction companies. The absorption of a number of unemployed persons from rural areas, and the creation of an expectation of such absorption has been important in orienting the Iban to the town as a new, exploitable niche. Many persons who come to Sibu looking for employment claim that there is no work for them in the rural areas. What actually is meant is that there is no work which they *want* to take up.

By 1947 the population of the Sibu urban area had reached 9,983 persons. The population trebled by 1960 to a total of 29,630, and the market area and the number of businesses doubled. Within the past fourteen years the population has more than doubled again, and shophouses have sprawled from the central trading area up and down the banks of the Rejang and Igan rivers.

The growth of Sibu as a trading center is due to a number of factors. We have described the products—jungle produce, rubber, timber, and pepper—which marked successive economic stages in the adaption of Iban to the Rejang Valley. These stages define the commercial history of Sibu, whose existence is inextricably bound to the hinterland. The rapid development of businesses during the past decade may be traced at least in part to the construction and extension of a road network, providing access of traders to agricultural products and much easier and cheaper travel for farmers who want to market their own produce. Trips from some rural areas that previously took half a day or more can now be made by taxi or public bus in half an hour.

Although Iban and other indigenes have contributed to the growth of Sibu through supplying produce and labor, few of them have owned shophouses or have run businesses in the town. Notable exceptions include Messrs. Unchat Chok and Jonathan Bangau, each of whom inherited a shophouse from his father. Chok, the late father of Unchat, was a close friend of the father of Mr. Wong Soon Kai, a distinguished Sibu surgeon, and was advised in his investments by the elder Wong. Chok and Bangau's father were among the Iban who refused to cut their rubber trees when the conflict between traditional rice cultivation and rubber gardening gave rise to the story of rubber eating rice. Both Bangau and Unchat have enjoyed a steady and considerable income from the rental of their shops. Bangau also is involved in several business enterprises, including serving as chairman of the Glass Sand Company, Ltd., which supplies sand for a Japanese firm and has an authorized capital of $250,000.

While few Iban are engaged actively in trade in Sibu, most of the Iban in the Sibu District and beyond have been affected by the dissemination of those values of the mercantile mentality expressed by Sibu traders. Iban are being drawn increasingly into the monetized economy of the market. Some commute to jobs, others daily bring in jungle ferns, areca nuts, or other marketable items. Many come to town for off-season occupations, others for more permanent employment.

Although many Iban are wage earners, few have been able to penetrate the tightly woven fabric of the Chinese-dominated business world, and it appears doubtful that many will for some time to come. The only apparent breakthrough has been in retailing fruit, vegetables, and occasionally poultry in the so-called Iban market or in some other unoccupied public space, realizing from the direct sale a much better return than by selling their goods to a Chinese middleman.

In the rural area, scores of Iban traders have emerged in the past two decades, running shophouses near their longhouse communities. In some instances these are new businesses where none previously existed. In other cases a business which formerly was handled by a Chinese trader has been taken over by an Iban shopkeeper. For example, in 1971 a Chinese shopkeeper in the upper reaches of the Salim River was forced to close his shop when he could not collect outstanding debts. With his departure, all of his former business fell to two Iban shopkeepers at Rumah Imba and Rumah Nyelang.

Sibu has emerged as a new niche with an important resource —cash. Sibu has grown through the input of rural produce and its exchange for foreign products. The importation of mass-produced goods which are both useful and prestigious has evoked desires among the Iban for outboard motors, sewing machines, pressure lamps, and the thousands of items available through trade. Whether Iban are frequent visitors to Sibu or see the town only once in a year or two, all are aware of the articles to be had there. And whereas more ambitious Iban formerly were "land-hungry" for the larger crops they could realize from new soil, current ambitious Iban may be described as "money-hungry" for the prestige and material comforts to be purchased with cash.

SERVICES, EDUCATION, RECRUITMENT, AND RECREATION

The growth of Sibu has been accompanied by the development of a number of services and facilities which are important to urban residents and attractive to rural people. We turn now to consider these facilities and their significance to the Iban.

Medical Services

Although the Rejang Valley cannot be called an inordinately unhealthy area, neither can it be described as disease-free. Early reports indicate that periodic outbreaks of smallpox, typhoid, malaria, and cholera occurred there. Respiratory diseases, the most serious being tuberculosis, are common. Health problems resulting from impure water supplies, viz. streams and wells, plague rural residents; gastrointestinal disorders such as diarrhea and dysentery occur frequently. The incidence of parasitic infection in the indigenous population is virtually universal.

In addition to gastroenteritis, tetanus continues to be a major cause of the relatively high rate of infant mortality in more remote Iban communities. In many cases tetanus results from the Iban's ritual cutting of the umbilical cord with an unsterilized bamboo sliver and the smearing of the navel with ashes that contain tetanus spores.

Despite the romanticized notions of some Westerners who see the "company manners" of Iban, Chinese, and others as an ideal condition of personal and social happiness, the plethora of terms for mental illness—which do not develop *in vacuo*—among the Iban, and the high incidence of hypertension among the Chinese betray the presence of psychic problems.

Attention has been given to the treatment of organic and functional illnesses as funds and personnel have been available. In 1902 a clinic and dispensary were built near Fort Brooke with a dresser in charge. This was expanded into a small hospital, but the response of Chinese and indigenes was slight, each group preferring its own traditional medical system.

In 1931, on the eve of his return to China, Lau King Howe, a prominent Chinese from a small village below Sibu, contributed one-half of the cost of a new hospital which still bears his name. The hospital has been enlarged and now contains ten wards. Exposure to the work of doctors and nurses in the hospital has elicited an ever-increasing response from members of all ethnic groups. During 1970, the last year for which figures indicating the ethnic group of patients were available, a total of 106,520 patients were treated in the hospital, as indicated in the table below.

Table 7-1 Number of patients treated at Lau King Howe Hospital, 1970

		Ethnic Group		Total of
	Chinese	Iban	Malay	All Cases
Number		40,243	34,237	32,040	106,520
New cases	46,050			
Follow-ups	54,404			
Admissions	6,066			
Total	106,520			

In addition to the government hospital, eight private doctors practice in the town. Although these doctors charge for their services and the medicines they dispense—in contrast to the socialized medicine of the hospital—they are visited by hundreds of patients each day. The proportion of patients who frequent private doctors is almost the same as those in the last table: 38 percent are Chinese, 32 percent are Iban, and 30 percent Malay.

The number of Iban patients is impressive because of the greater distance and difficulty of access which they face. Although the psychotherapy of Iban shamanism is highly developed, Iban *materia medica* is limited to the use of certain fruits, such as the sago palm which is used to treat diarrhea, leaves for burns, and grasses for wounds. Thus the Iban have been attracted by the techniques and pharmacopoeia of the hospital staff and private doctors. It is not uncommon for some Iban to solicit treatment both in the hospital and from a private practitioner in the same morning, particularly if he is refused an injection in the hospital. So deep is the faith of many Iban in the magic of the needle that on occasion they will go to two doctors on the same day to get injections, not telling the second that they have been treated by the first. The rationale is that if one shot does some good, two will be doubly beneficial.

In 1955 a maternity clinic providing antenatal and postnatal care for mothers and infants was begun. A majority of women receiving help there are Chinese, but an increasing number of Iban women are availing themselves of the clinic's services.

Another medical service that has assumed importance is the Family Planning Clinic. Begun in 1963, the clinic deals with almost 15,000 women annually. Iban response was slow at first due to a lack of understanding of the work of the clinic, but in 1970 Iban women constituted the largest single ethnic group that visited the clinic. The clinic is popular among married Iban women who want to avoid pregnancies, during which wives fear that their husbands will be unfaithful. The clinic is also popular among the unmarried Iban women who, for reasons we shall discuss later, have come to Sibu for prostitution and simply want to avoid becoming pregnant.

Table 7–2 Sibu Family Planning Clinic Attendance, 1964–1970

Year	Chinese	Malay	Iban	Others	Total
			New		
1964	296	121	41	11	369
1965	742	98	143	14	997
1966	637	57	235	27	956
1967	612	40	307	27	986
1968	488	68	518	13	1,087
1969	382	89	477	16	964
1970	338	67	374	10	789
Total	3,495	440	2,095	118	6,148
			Repeat		
1964	242	30	32	9	313
1965	2,651	380	449	44	3,524
1966	3,770	545	987	118	5,420
1967	5,335	713	1,838	209	8,095
1968	6,446	972	3,307	217	10,942
1969	5,941	1,454	4,474	149	12,018
1970	5,163	1,710	6,062	94	13,029
Total	29,548	5,804	17,149	840	53,341

Source: Family Planning Association, 1970 report, Sibu Branch, Sarawak, p. 2.

Welfare Agencies

Since the Second World War, a number of welfare agencies have been started in Sibu. The functions of these agencies are new and little understood by the Iban community, and some are as yet culturally unacceptable to them. For example, in the two homes for the aged at Salim and Bukit Lima, only two of the seventy-three inmates are Iban, the remainder being Chinese. Asked about placing old people in the homes, one Iban man said that it was unthinkable, for as long as they were able they would care for their own. Iban social security is still based upon strong ties of kinship and does not yet permit consideration of institutions such as the homes for the aged.

By far the most important agency to the Iban is the Welfare Department which in 1971 provided rice to residents in about one-half of the longhouses in the Sibu District. The amount of rice granted to each family was relatively small—on the average enough for two weeks—but the expectations born by the grants have been enormous. Seeing the bags of rice coming from government stores or Chinese shops upon authorization of a welfare officer, the Iban have been convinced that food supplies in town are more dependable than those produced in the country. One government official acknowledged that though recipients are told that the grant is given but once, they anticipate being able to obtain rice from the government annually. A further implication of the grant is that Iban who previously would not have thought of demeaning themselves by asking for rice, now are determined to "get their own" if others are receiving grants. In 1972 many Iban families ran out of rice and made new requests the cost of which was estimated by an officer of the Welfare Department to exceed $50,000.

Education

The first schools in the area of Sibu were privately supported and run by Chinese settlers. Between 1904 and 1911 the second Rajah's government provided funds for the starting of a number of small schools in the outstations. Although Charles Brooke favored a limited education system for selected Iban, he never implemented his ideas, and what education was provided for them was entirely in mission schools: Anglican, Roman Catholic, and Methodist.

In the Rejang Valley education remained an almost entirely urban activity until 1928 when aid was requested for beginning a school in the Iban community at Bawang Assan. It is not surprising that the first request from an Iban community of the Sibu District for a school should have been from Bawang Assan, given the exposure of this community to Chinese and European officers of the Brooke administration.

Schools were established slowly in Iban communities, and by 1950 there were only four Local Authority Iban Schools in the Sibu District. The attitude of many Iban was, "We didn't go to school, and we can make a living. Why should our children go to school?" On the other hand, the Rajahs were reluctant to proliferate schools and Western-style education for fear that the "genius of Iban culture" would be destroyed. Hence, Iban education was restricted to seven years.

Following the cession of Sarawak from the Brookes to the British in 1946, the Colonial Government was pressed for educated personnel to fill its staff, and Iban with as little as four years of elementary education were selected for teachers' training and employment. Those students who passed the Common Entrance Examination, given at the end of the sixth grade, went on to the secondary schools, all of which at that time were located in the main towns. The most prestigious ones were in Sibu and Kuching. Students who passed the Sarawak Junior Examination after the ninth grade, or Senior Cambridge after the eleventh grade, were guaranteed employment either with the government or companies.

By the mid-1950s the relationship between education and employment had been perceived by many Iban parents, and the rush was on for schools. By 1958 schools had been built in sixteen Iban communities, and as many more longhouse groups were clamoring for them. Similarly, in the towns it soon became apparent that the government-aided schools could not handle the increasing numbers of students wanting to attend secondary school, and demands were made for permission to open private, government-approved but unaided, secondary schools. By 1962 five unaided secondary schools had been started in Sibu, taking students who did not pass the Common Entrance Examination and were denied entrance to government-aided schools. The equation of education and employment has been held to tenaciously by Iban parents, many of whom sacrificially pay fifteen to twenty dollars each month in anticipation of future rewards through their children's employment.

Those children who have been selected to attend government-aided secondary schools have until recently had a better educational experience and chance for passing the higher-level examinations. (This generalization is no longer valid, however, for the results of some private secondary schools have been better than those of aided schools for the past two years.) Of 143 Iban who studied in aided secondary schools between 1960 and 1970, all either are employed or are spouses of wage earners. None of these 143 students has returned to take up residence in his longhouse. By contrast, the results and employment opportunities for students in unaided schools have tended to be more disappointing both to the youngsters and to their parents, so that some students in this group do return to the longhouse.

The effects of education on Iban have been varied. Education has helped to reinforce the changing value system from "the good life of rice farming" to "the better life of employment" by offering a means to its attainment. The initial location of all secondary schools in urban centers led to a radical disorientation of young people to their culture and disengagement from their society, so that many have refused to return to the longhouse and some who have tried have found themselves unaccepted and ill-equipped to compete with their peers.

In a perceptive statement on the effects of education on Iban society, an officer of the Education Department wrote that

the basic weakness of Iban education is that it is regarded by parents, children, teachers, and all concerned, not as preparation for life in an Iban community, but as a means of escaping it. . . . The gap between schoolhouse and longhouse yawns even wider; the situation was well epitomized by a certain teacher's crushing rebuke of a bad boy . . . "You are good for nothing but to be a farmer" (*Sarawak Gazette,* December 31, 1962, page 269).

Given the expectations of parents and students, relatively highly educated young people return to the longhouse to visit, but not to live. Despite the government's policy urging them "back-to-the-country," young Iban may be expected to continue to escape the country and to seek new ways of living in urban areas.

Recruitment

From the late nineteenth century, Iban from the Sibu District and other parts of the Rejang Valley have traveled to work as far afield as New Guinea. Tuba, a famous bard from Bawang Assan, signed on with a company in Malacca, and upon completion of his contract, signed on with another company and worked for one year in New Guinea.

Not all Iban are so adventurous nor so inclined to wander so far in search of work. The expansion of Sibu and other towns has permitted many more to find employment and adventure closer to home. The number of Iban who moved into Sibu during the first half of this century was relatively small because there were few opportunities open to them, and in addition the Brooke Raj discouraged their movements. With the development of Sibu during the past twenty-five years, more and more Iban are seeking employment in or through the town.

In 1970 I conducted a survey of 200 Iban residents in the urban area. Of the sample, 171 were employed and the other twenty-nine were housewives. The 171 persons were employed in thirty-five different occupations, as indicated in the table on page 164.

More highly educated Iban are employed by the government, administrative councils, political parties, banks, companies, and churches. Employment with these organizations provides a steady income and security, both of which are highly valued. Even Iban in low-paying jobs are envied their positions, and there is pressure on every salaried Iban to be alert to job opportunities for kinsmen. As in traditional society, factionalism and nepotism are by no means dead nor are they considered vices. Rather, they are recognized practices which are considered essential if a person is to have a chance at getting a job. For example, when a position was created by one of the councils, there were more than one hundred applications for the single job. The man who was eventually chosen was by his own admission no better qualified than many other applicants, but he had a friend on the selection committee.

Iban who are fortunate enough to be employed by government, company, or church often plan their future in Sibu—despite their statements to the effect that they want to return to the longhouse, few actually do. By contrast, Iban who are employed as day laborers, as trishaw drivers, or as bar-girls and/or prostitutes seldom take up long-term residence in town. On an average, workers in the latter categories remain in town between one and two years at the most.

Special mention must be made about the young Iban women who appear in the table as waitresses, bar-girls, and "self-employed females." An estimated three hundred such women work as prostitutes; they are recruited by madams—some of whom are from Singapore, by friends who already are working in town, or they are enlisted by male companions. Given the casual attitude toward sex, the position of relative equality which women enjoy in their society, but the limited number of economic opportunities—other than the brunt of rice-farming which falls to them—it is not surprising that some young Iban

Table 7–3 A sample of economically active Iban Sibu, 1970

Category	Number Employed	Self-employed
Government:		
Cooperative Officers	2	
Medical Doctors	2	
Lab Technicians	2	
Other Medical Work	11	
District Officer	1	
Prison Warden	1	
Public Works	3	
Teachers/Education Department	4	
Agriculture	4	
Telecommunications	1	
Customs	1	
Police, Rangers	29	
Overseas Survey	1	
Civil Defense	1	
Councils:		
Secretary	1	
Clerk	1	
Midwife	1	
Political Parties	4	
Banks, Trades, Companies:		
Office Boys	2	
Import-Export Clerk	1	
Construction Laborers	20	
Waitresses, Bar Girls	11	
Piling Operators	3	
Theater Ushers, Projectionists	3	
Brickworks Laborer	1	
Electricity Company	1	
Custodians	2	
Cooks, Maids	5	
Females, "Self-employed"		25
Trishaw Drivers		10
Church:		
Literature Production	2	
Ministers	8	
Gardeners	4	
TOTALS	133	35

women have found the money and other material rewards of the town more attractive than their future in the longhouse.

Recreation

"Why did I move to Sibu?" answered the young man. "It's more exciting, there are more people, and you can meet more people here than in the longhouse."

Recreational activities have been important in attracting Iban to town. Early records indicate that by the turn of the century hundreds of Iban participated in or watched boat races held during the Christmas regatta. The regatta provided a reason—if one were needed—for Iban to leave their work and come to town where they could meet Chinese, Malays, Indians, and Europeans, eat and drink, and see the lights and crowds. Although the last regatta in Sibu was held a decade ago, there currently are many other pleasures which Sibu has to offer rural visitors.

The town boasts five movie theaters, all of which do a good business in a town not yet serviced by television. The movies that are seen are an important means of disseminating new ideas and values. By far the most popular movies among the Iban are Hindustani films, war stories, and cowboy/adventure stories.

The simple pleasure of meeting friends and having a drink or a meal in one of the numerous coffee shops is probably the major attraction. From early morning until closing time, the coffee shops along Channel Road do a brisk business with an Iban clientele.

All forms of gambling are popular, from the Social Welfare Department's lotteries to a small game of cards. More than any other single form of gambling, however, cockfighting probably attracts more Iban and Chinese men. In the town, men stake their prized roosters out on traffic islands, carry them proudly under their arms as they bicycle through the streets, preen their feathers, and sneak in an illegal cockfight whenever they think the heads of the police are turned the other way.

On Sundays and holidays, cockfights are arranged by the purchase of a license from the District Office. In an interesting case of economic cooperation, Iban headmen from the Oya Road area purchase the licenses in turn—one headman one week, another the next, and so on until each has had a turn. The license holder and his helpers receive a part of the gate and of all bets placed.

By the judgment of some Iban who have been to Kuching or Singapore, the town of Sibu and even smaller ports are limited in recreational facilities. The towns nevertheless hold attractions for Iban of the Sibu District and beyond who are looking for diversion from their work and play.

SETTLEMENT PATTERNS: IBAN IN TOWN

Within the past decade more than 3,000 Iban have moved into the town of Sibu. Whereas the Brookes discouraged the movement of Iban to Sarawak's towns, and the population of Sibu included only 693 Iban (2 percent) in 1960, in 1970 Iban residents numbered between 3,000 and 4,000 (8 percent) of the urban population. (Although administrators declined to include the Lanang Road Field Force in their consideration of the Iban population in Sibu, the exposure to and effects of the urban center as a type of adaptation upon members of the Field Force and their families are incontrovertible.)

The Iban who have moved into Sibu have in some cases been "pushed" into town, and in others, "pulled" by perceived attractions and hopes. We have noted the natural problems that confront the farmer: the generally poor soil conditions that exist in many areas; the unpredictable climate with unseasonable flooding downriver (as in August 1971), and prolonged dry seasons in some upriver areas (as in September 1972); the firm belief of the indigenous population that double-cropping of rice will not be done; and the fluctuations of market prices on rubber and other cash crops.

It is difficult to exaggerate the contrast in yields between communities participating in the Padi Planting Scheme and those planting dry rice. Rumah Nyala is representative of the longhouses in the Sibu District which have achieved a high percentage of self-sufficiency in rice production. By contrast, the families in Rumah Gaong and those in the hillier regions of the Song and Kapit Districts are rarely able to produce enough rice to last from one harvest to the next. In response to a survey conducted by Schwenk in the upriver area, the universal response to the question, "What is the greatest need in your community?" was, "To increase rice production" (cf. Schwenk, 1974).

The problematic character of rice production has led to the disillusionment of some Iban, especially the young. Talking about the time, labor, and hope invested in his fields, only to receive a poor crop as his return, one farmer complained wearily: "What's the use? We plant at the right time. We observe the rituals and make the appropriate offerings—and it's in vain!"

Rice production is not only problematic; it also is just plain hard work. The excitement and air of romantic adventure that marks the beginning of the agricultural year soon gives way to aching muscles and bone-deep weariness. Men and women arise at four o'clock in the morning to go to their fields from which they return at sundown. Even in downriver areas, the soil often must be prepared with the use of a *pito* or chopping blade, the use of which hour after hour in the hot sun is exhausting and painful. It is small wonder that Iban men customarily have left the task of weeding to women and have gone traveling after the fields have been planted.

The fall of rubber prices over the past two years has made the situation of many Iban critical. Unable to produce enough rice and forced to purchase this staple, Iban have become heavily dependent upon cash derived principally from the sale of rubber. When the price of the low-grade rubber—unsmoked sheet or Grade Five—which most Iban produce fell to two to three cents per pound, all except those who had no alternative stopped tapping their trees and sought cash elsewhere.

In contrast to the hard work necessary to produce rice, Iban perceive in the towns stores of abundant stocks to be had with much less effort. In fact, one Iban stated that the compelling factor in his decision to move to Sibu was the dependability of the food supply. Mat, a headman from Langup, a community twenty minutes downriver from Sibu, said that he would like to move to Sibu for the same reason, but had no education and was fearful that he could not find work.

That all Iban do not share his fears is evident in the large number who work in Sibu. These Iban may be divided into two groups with respect to their settlement patterns and their presence in Sibu: commuters and residents. We now shall consider these two groups in turn.

Commuters

The principal characteristic of Iban who travel in and out of Sibu daily to work is their proximity to the town. Workers from Rumah Nyala use bicycles over a path past Sungai Merah into Sibu. From Nanga Assan, Langup, Bidut, and other nearby areas, workers use launches or small ferries, bringing their bicycles with them or using the bus service near the jetty. About one dozen Iban men drive private taxis from the Oya and Durin Roads, bringing in passengers from their home communities and other fares that they pick up along the road.

Distance is the critical criterion which determines whether workers commute or move into town. Although transportation is available for greater distances than those described above, the cost of the fare is prohibitive so that persons from more remote areas find it cheaper to rent a room for ten dollars per month.

Commuters include both men and women, young and old. Men predominate in various types of work offering regular employment, such as gardening, construction, brickyard labor, clerical service, and janitorial. With few exceptions, most men who commute are employed in unskilled jobs with relatively low wages. Most women who commute are best described as self-employed, selling vegetables in the Iban market or working as bar-girls. Of the fifty-five members of Rumah Nyala who are wage earners, seventeen commute daily to Sibu. Fifteen of the commuters are men and two are women.

It is among commuters and their families that the advantages of rural settlements near the town are realized. In these families women do most of the farm work and men supplement the family's income with wages. Unlike permanent residents in Sibu, among whom both husband and wife live in town and depend upon the husband's income, the families of commuters have achieved a division of labor which permits maximization of the productive potential of both sexes. Because these families do not have to buy their rice and at the same time have cash to buy other food and prestige items, they are generally more affluent than those families that depend upon either agriculture or wages for their subsistence.

In Rumah Nyala, Imba, and Gaong, the shophouses are maintained by commuters, or other members of their families. The shopkeepers, who work in Sibu, use their daily trips to purchase goods for their shops as well as to dispose of any produce which they may have purchased from members of their communities. The success of each of these shops may be attributed to the diversification of activities—farming, wage earning, and shopkeeping—so that the families have other resources upon which they can call if one or the other fails them.

Residents

The Iban who have moved into Sibu have, for the most part, scattered throughout the town. Their residences are related to a number of factors, the most important being the presence or absence of a kinsman, the length of time they plan to stay in town, the position and amount of income, and whether quarters are furnished by the employer.

It must be made clear that there is no "Iban Ward" in the town of Sibu, nor any settlement pattern remotely resembling a longhouse. The heaviest concentrations of Iban are at the Lanang Road Field Force Camp, where an average of 1,000 troops, mostly Iban, live with their families. Until 1972 Iban in the Malaysian Rangers were housed together with their families in apartment buildings of the Sungai Antu Industrial Area, a development on the north bank of the Igan below Sibu. The Rangers have since been moved to their camp on Oya Road. Iban tend to follow Iban, however, and several hundred families still live in the Industrial Area.

A vast majority of Iban residents live either in rented quarters or in housing furnished by their employers. Seventy-three of the Iban in our sample of 200 urban residents live in quarters provided by their employer. Forty-seven of these employees are renting rooms, and 22 indicated that they are living with friends or kinsmen.

In several visits to the now-razed "Iban Guest House" I discovered that only those Iban who knew no single person in Sibu stayed there. Some were staying there to visit sick relatives in the hospital, others were working temporarily or more permanently, and were saving money by living in the Guest House. As soon as they could find other lodging that their resources permitted them to rent, however, they moved out to take up other accommodations. From then on, these new residents were subject to demands for hospitality from their kinsmen and friends.

Of the Iban surveyed, only nine of the 171 economically active persons owned their own homes. All homeowners have been longtime residents in Sibu, and generally they are more affluent than those living in rented quarters or those furnished by the employer. The small number of Iban homeowners reflects the inflated prices of land and houses in Sibu, and probably the indecision that most urban Iban feel about their future, i.e., whether they will remain in the town or return to the longhouse community.

SUMMARY

The port towns of Sarawak, of which Sibu is representative, have become landmarks of importance in the lives of the Iban, new niches to which they are adapting. From such towns the lives of the Iban are administered. In such towns, Iban trade, send their youth for education, accept employment, and find opportunities for recreation. While the contacts of most Iban with the towns and their residents still are irregular, these centers figure prominently in the world of the Iban. Some Iban have discovered in the towns not only places to visit, but new sites for settlement.

Chapter 8

A WORLD INSIDE OUT

The Copernican revolution occurred for the Iban within the past century. Prior to and even during much of that period the Iban were secure in their position at the center of their universe. Structurally and ritually, the longhouse was the focal point of their world. Other peoples were defined as they related to the Iban, who expanded to bring them within the sphere of true humanity.

All of this has changed through the events of the late nineteenth and twentieth centuries. The Iban no longer are secure at the center of their universe, for many are anxious about what they perceive as their marginality. Not only is the longhouse no longer the focal point of their world, but many question its future as a viable residence type. Whereas the Iban previously expanded to assimilate other peoples, they are now expanding into urban areas and being brought within the sphere of modern cultures.

Put simply, the Iban who once were the dominant group on Borneo have been subjected to successively more assertive administrations—Brooke, British, and Malaysian—and assailed by countless influences, all from "another world." As they have responded to these external forces their adaptive strategies and behavior have changed so that the formerly integrated and interdependent elements of the Iban world are being transformed.

In this chapter we shall examine the principal changes that have taken place in Iban society and culture, noting the virtual abandonment of some features and the persistence of others. The Iban have gained greater control of productive resources, and have discovered new resources, such as cash, education, and employment, so that their "need" of one another is now different.

The new world of the Iban is not being created *ex nihilo*, but rather from the materials and symbols which constituted the old. The world of the Iban, as that of other peoples, has probably never been fixed and static, but in flux and dynamic. The new phenomenon, however, that is most obvious is what has been called "the pluralization of life worlds," so that the Iban are being exposed to different patterns of behavior and beliefs, new messages and meanings, and a vastly more complex array of values and expectations from which to choose. The Iban are not victims of confusion and disorder, subjects of what Edmund Leach has called *A Runaway World?*. They still order their world—through the recasting of their categories and the reorganization of their institutions.

THE *BILIK*-FAMILY

The *bilik*-family remains the basic unit of Iban society. Accommodation to altered circumstances and alien examples, however, have led to developments which are changing the profile and functions of the *bilik*-family.

We discussed four principles of recruitment to the family. Of these, birth continues to be common and incorporation rare. New developments, however, are affecting practices of adoption and marriage, and we shall analyze these two principles in turn.

Adoption traditionally has been an important practice by which children have been distributed within Iban society, those families having too many giving to those having none. The main function of such an adoption practice was to provide a child to care for childless adults when they became aged or infirm.

Adoption has declined significantly in those longhouse communities which are closer to urban centers. Indeed, there is a direct relationship between distance from the town and incidence of adoption. The total number of adoptions per long-house are significantly lower in my sample of communities in the Sibu District than the number and average for the Iban of the more remote Kapit District (cf. Freeman, 1970: 17). In the houses on which I concentrated there were two adoptions in Rumah Nyala, five in Rumah Imba, seven in Rumah Nyelang, and thirteen in Rumah Gaong, although the number of families in the four houses varies only from twenty-seven to thirty.

It seems to me that changes in the rate of adoption are due to one principal factor, viz. a much lower incidence of childlessness or much greater control over pregnancies and childbirth. Iban women in the Sibu District, especially in Rumah Nyala and other acculturated communities, have greater control over pregnancies through the use of contraceptives. As a consequence the number of pregnancies among Iban women of the Sibu District is only about one-half that of Iban women in the Kapit District. Yet, ironically, the profile of the Sibu Iban is a much younger one. Through hospitals and clinics there has been a massive dissemination of information on the care of mothers and children, so that pregnant Iban women in the Sibu District have a greater probability of a full-term carriage. There also is much better prenatal and postnatal care for infants and mothers, together with the abandonment of the overly restrictive diets on nursing mothers and the ritual cutting of the umbilical cord—using bamboo and ash—resulting in a spectacular decline in infant mortality as well as the premature aging of women in their twenties. In contrast to the infant mortality rate of approximately 50 percent—the average in remote communities—there was not a single death of an infant or child in Rumah Nyala during the 1960s.

Thus, adoption, which has been an important mechanism for binding families together, has diminished considerably. Yet childless couples, for example in Rumah Nyala, are an exception.

Patterns of marriage and postmarital residence also are changing in response to the new environment to which the Iban are adapting. Marriage has been considered a means of creating or strengthening ties between families and kin-groups, of balancing need and labor, and of guaranteeing care for parents.

Although Iban adults almost unanimously affirmed their belief that marriages should take place between members of the same kin-group—to retain control of productive resources—and within the same community—to maintain control of the resident population—in practice marriages today commonly take place between members of different groups and communities. In Rumah Nyala, for example, only seven of thirty-one marriages were between members of the same kin-group. Only four were in-house. Commenting on the preference for marriages with men and women outside one's own longhouse, several expressed a reticence to marry a member of one's own community. As one put it, "The new is the more satisfying."

Among the Sibu Iban, marriage is looked upon less as an alliance between kin-groups and more as a private arrangement between the parties concerned. For this reason, the number of marriages arranged by parents is negligible. In Rumah Nyala only one marriage was negotiated by the parents of the couple, all others having been arranged by the man and the woman. In thirteen cases the couple consulted their parents prior to reaching a decision to marry, but in the other seventeen cases there was no consultation.

This spirit of independence with respect to marriage is particularly clear among more highly educated Iban. Education below the ninth grade seems to have little or no effect on marriages. For Iban who study in the ninth grade and above, however, it appears to have a radical effect. Just as high school education gives the young Iban greater latitude in selection of jobs, so too does it allow independence in marriage and the family. In a survey that I conducted among Iban who studied in the high schools of Sibu between 1960 and 1970, 137 of the 143 students who responded indicated that they wanted to choose their own spouses. Less than one-half were inclined toward any consultation with their parents.

Higher education results in later marriages. A majority of Iban marry between the ages of fifteen and seventeen years. Of my survey of former Iban high school students, 102 were unmarried at age twenty. One-half of the students had been out of school for three or more years and expressed a desire to defer the responsibilities of marriage until they felt themselves financially "set."

All of the respondents indicated that they wanted a spouse who was at least literate. Thirty-four stated that they wanted a partner who was as well educated as themselves.

None of the respondents have taken up residence in a long-house—consonant with the socially disengaging and culturally reorienting effects of education. All live near the place of their employment. This augurs a universal practice of neolocal residence among highly educated Iban, and a model which may become increasingly emulated.

We have noted earlier that parental arrangement of marriage was an attempt to maintain social levels in Iban society, especially avoiding marriages with the descendants of slaves or with persons who were supposed to have the power to hex. Education has eradicated such stigma, for the economic potential of a highly educated person takes precedence over both low-class status and an accursed background. The educated and hence potentially employable young person is acceptable as a spouse, even to the most highly status-conscious parents.

The ecology of the Sibu Iban has resulted in changes in the profile of postmarital residence. In his research among the Iban of the Sut River, Freeman (1970: 23) found residences almost uniformly ambilocal (i.e., "either location"). This almost equal incidence of residence with husband's or wife's family is probably related to the roles played by males and females in shifting cultivation. This probability gains support from the residence patterns in Rumah Gaong and other communities in my sample where shifting cultivation is still the farming technique.

In Rumah Nyala and Imba, however, whose members practice wet rice, permanent field agriculture, and many of whom are employed in Sibu or elsewhere, there is a predominance of uxorilocal residence, i.e., of men joining their wives' families. Of forty-nine marriages in Rumah Nyala and forty-four in Rumah Imba, twenty-six and twenty-eight, respectively, were uxorilocal.

This change in postmarital residence patterns may be due to two principal factors. First, women have come to play a greater role in wet rice farming than they did in shifting cultivation, important though their role was in the hills. Among the Iban of the houses mentioned, if labor exchange is arranged, the women do it among themselves and preferably with female kin.

In hiring labor, women contract the employees, whether men or women. Even if no labor is exchanged and no hiring is done, the women still express a preference for working their fields near their own kin rather than with strangers or even affines.

A second reason is that an increasing number of Iban men are taking up employment away from their longhouses, especially in some downriver communities. In such situations, patrilocal residence is problematic and the wife may prefer to remain in her natal *bilik* or to follow her husband and live neolocally.

Iban marriages traditionally have been invariably monogamous. Divorce was common so that men and women married frequently, but never with more than one spouse at a time. In the lower Rejang, however, where Iban have been exposed to the marriage patterns of Malays and Chinese, six cases of sororal polygyny (two sisters marrying the same man) and eight cases of nonsororal polygyny (two unrelated women marrying the same man) were discovered. In the six cases of sororal polygyny, the men involved were either headmen or relatively wealthy. The women who became second wives all had been widowed prior to taking up residence with her sister and husband. What emerges from these cases is an example of "social security" for the widowed second wife in an alien marriage form adopted by the Iban. In telling me about his second wife, Tuai Rumah Nyambang said that "After my sister-in-law, my second wife, was widowed, our kin-groups met and discussed the problem of her support and agreed that it would be suitable for her to be my second wife."

Unlike the families in which sororal polygyny occurs, in which the wives share a common residence with their husband, in the cases of nonsororal polygyny the wives live in separate residences. One *tuai rumah* was married for about ten years before he took his second wife. His first wife lives in a longhouse and his second wife in a rented house in Sibu.

Commenting on these deviant forms of marriage, Ganai of Rumah Nyala said with obvious disapproval and with a feeling of weariness brought on by many changes in his lifetime, "In former times, we couldn't have more than one wife at a time. This [having two wives] is a new thing, copying the Chinese and Malays. This is something that has happened since Malaysia."

THE LONGHOUSE

Longhouse residence remains culturally normative for the Iban, even for those who have long since moved into town. We noted earlier the comments of the Sibu Iban who has lived away from the longhouse for more than three decades, yet contends that the longhouse is the proper place for the Iban. Thus you may take the Iban out of his longhouse but—at least in this case—you cannot take belief in the value of longhouse living out of the Iban.

Longhouses continue to be social and ceremonial centers. The major rites of passage for most Iban are still observed in the longhouse. Urbanized Iban return on the occasion of important rituals.

The longhouse remains a symbol of unity and integration by which non-kin are made "kinsmen." While Freeman generally is correct in observing that a family does not take up residence in a longhouse unless either the husband or wife has kinsmen there (1970: 102), there are exceptions, such as Ili and his family who can count no "real" kinsmen in Rumah Nyala.

Not only can Ili count no kinsmen in Rumah Nyala, but both he and Geranding are members of other ethnic groups! The relative ease of attachment to the longhouse has encouraged Melanau, Memaloh, Chinese, and others who have friends in Iban communities to join the longhouse to which they are readily admitted.

Rumah Nyala, Aup, was founded three generations ago, in about 1910, by a small group of kinsmen comprising two brothers and three cousins. Members of twenty-four of the thirty-three families of Rumah Nyala trace their descent from the founding kin-group, so that in describing their community, one spokesman said, "We of Aup are all of one kin-group."

In order to test the veracity of this statement, I plotted the incidence of interrelatedness of the thirty-three families in Rumah Nyala. If every family were related to all of the others, the total number of relationships would be 528, i.e., $(33 \times 32)/2$. That such is not the case is apparent from an examination of Table 8–1.

Several important changes have taken place in the traditional longhouse. First, in contrast to the formerly impermanent

Table 8–1 *Bilik*-families: incidence of interrelatedness, Rumah Nyala, Sungai Aup

Vari-able	1	2	3	4	5	6	7	8	9	10	11	12	13	14	15	16	17	18	19	20	21	22	23	24	25	26	27	28	29	30	31	32	33
2	x																																
3	x	x																															
4		x	x																														
5	x	x	x																														
6					x																												
7					x	x																											
8	x	x	x	x	x	x	x																										
9	x	x	x	x	x	x	x	x																									
10	x	x	x	x	x	x	x	x	x																								
11	x	x	x	x	x	x	x	x	x	x																							
12	x	x	x	x	x	x	x	x	x	x	x																						
13	x	x	x	x	x	x	x	x	x	x	x	x																					
14	x	x	x	x	x	x	x	x	x	x	x	x	x																				
15	x	x	x	x	x	x	x	x	x	x	x	x	x	x																			
16	x	x	x	x	x	x	x	x	x	x	x	x	x	x	x																		
17	x	x	x	x	x	x	x	x	x	x	x	x	x	x	x	x																	
18	x	x	x	x	x	x	x	x	x	x	x	x	x	x	x	x	x																

Table 8–1 (continued)

Variable	1	2	3	4	5	6	7	8	9	10	11	12	13	14	15	16	17	18	19	20	21	22	23	24	25	26	27	28	29	30	31	32	33
19	x	x	x		x			x	x	x	x	x	x	x	x	x	x	x															
20										x																							
21										x										x													
22										x										x	x												
23	x	x	x		x			x	x	x	x	x	x	x	x	x	x	x	x														
24	x	x	x		x			x	x	x	x	x	x	x	x	x	x	x	x				x										
25	x	x	x		x			x	x	x	x	x	x	x	x	x	x	x	x				x	x									
26	x	x	x		x			x	x	x	x	x	x	x	x	x	x	x	x				x	x	x								
27	x	x	x		x			x	x	x	x	x	x	x	x	x	x						x	x	x	x							
28	x	x	x								x		x														x						
29	x	x	x		x			x	x	x	x	x	x	x	x	x	x	x	x				x	x	x	x	x	x					
30																																	
31				x																													
32										x										x	x	x											
33	x	x	x		x			x	x	x	x	x	x	x	x	x	x	x					x	x	x	x	x	x	x				

x = relation between families

structures, built to stand a decade or so, modern longhouses are built to last. The permanence of modern longhouses attests to the fact that the Iban feel themselves "here to stay," having adopted permanent field cultivation and cash crops such as rubber and pepper. Until the beginning of this century, the longhouses of migrants to the Rejang Valley were constructed of materials which were soon ravaged by weather and insects, consonant with the practice of shifting cultivation. The construction of the first permanent structure in the Lower Rejang, the legendary *Rumah Papan* ("House of Planks"), was such a significant development that it is still remembered by older Iban of the Bawang Assan area.

New longhouses represent sizable investments of time and money. Local materials, such as ironwood or other hardwoods, are used for supporting posts, joists, and shingles, and are combined with hardboard, asbestos tiles, and zinc sheeting to provide sturdy, durable buildings. (Although zinc sheets are considered prestigious, they are poor roofing material for the tropics. Once, following a long boat trip which required much pulling of the boat over the shallows, I was seated beneath such a roof and felt as if I were in a sauna!)

In addition to new farming techniques which have made the rotation of fields unnecessary, the permanence of downriver longhouse settlements has been influenced by other circumstances as well. In some cases, Iban have been forced to settle permanently in areas where they have been surrounded by Chinese. Although not all of the land in the Sibu District has been surveyed, none can be described as unclaimed. Thus, for want of other land to which they can move, the Iban have become encircled by Chinese. In one case with which I am familiar this has been largely the doing of the Iban themselves. The people of Rumah Lubang on the Oya Road sold much of their land to Chinese for a quick profit in the form of a new, carpenter-built longhouse. Having divested themselves of most of their land, they now are "stuck" on the little they have left.

Because of their inexperience of working with foreign materials, and reflecting the growing specialization noted in the previous chapter, Iban more frequently are hiring Malay or Chinese carpenters to construct new longhouses. For example, most of the central units in Rumah Nyala, Nyelang, and Imba were built of planed boards, asbestos sheets for ceilings, and commercial shingles, and built by non-Iban carpenters.

A second change in the longhouse community is in its elaboration, both internally and externally. We have described the units of the traditional longhouse—porch, verandah, family room, and loft. In an increasing number of houses guest rooms *(tiko)* are built off the verandah of the headman or other prominent families. This structural innovation was found at three of the four longhouses in my study; only Rumah Gaong, the more conservative community, lacked a *tiko.* At Rumah Imba, for example, there are two such rooms, both fitted with sliding iron-grill doors which are locked when the *tiko* is not in use. At Rumah Nyelang, the *tiko* was separated from the *ruai* by a folding door. These rooms have been built to accommodate guests whom Iban are reluctant to have stay in their family rooms, feeling that more honor—and sophistication—is shown to the guests by providing them with their own quarters.

Iban communities traditionally have included the longhouse dwelling. Thus, for example, Rumah Gaong is a single house with several attached dwellings *(pelaboh)* at the edge of the porch. Diversification of activities has led to a proliferation of outbuildings, which now surround many longhouses. Each of the four communities studied, and twenty of the thirty-seven surveyed, had a shophouse conveniently located nearby where matches, sugar, salt, and canned goods such as milk, meat, and fish are exchanged for rubber and pepper. Again, interestingly, Enchul's shop at Rumah Gaong is attached to the porch. Other buildings, such as smokehouses for processing rubber, and in some communities separate buildings for livestock, complete the settlements. A layout of the community of Rumah Nyala is provided on the following page.

A third change in residence patterns is in the fragmentation of some longhouses to build individual dwellings. We have seen that the breakup of longhouses to construct new multifamily dwellings is an old practice. When Iban communities had "farmed out" land at a convenient distance, they broke up, some families remaining, others moving on to pioneer new areas. In addition to longhouse fragmentation to permit communities to regroup, a new reason for longhouse fragmentation

Figure 8. The Rumah Nyala community.

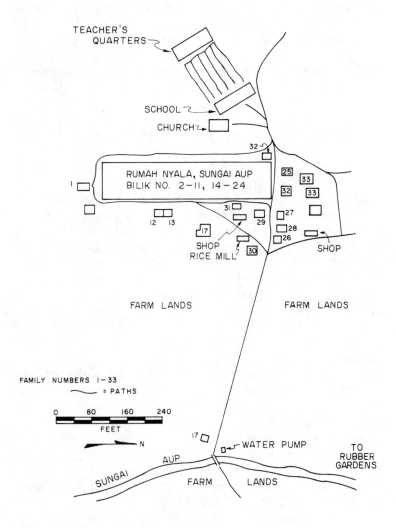

is now appearing in the Rejang Valley, viz. the construction of permanent individual dwellings.

During the past decade, ten of the thirty-seven longhouses in my sample were dismantled or abandoned by their residents. In six of the cases the families rebuilt according to the longhouse pattern. In four of the cases, however, the Iban did not construct a new longhouse but rather a cluster of individual houses. The members of Pengulu Poh's house on the Pasai River dismantled their house and built separate dwellings on the knoll where their longhouse formerly stood. The people of Rumah Buda left their old longhouse to build separate houses alongside the road.

A number of reasons have been suggested by Iban to account for the permanent abandonment of longhouses. Headhunting is no longer practiced, so defense is no longer a necessity. Permanent-field agriculture does not require the concentration of a male labor force for clearing virgin forests. The introduction of the Padi Planting Scheme by the Agriculture Department has permitted approximately 60 percent of the Iban in the district to farm within one mile of their houses. Some Iban consider the longhouse a fire hazard: when a fire breaks out in one apartment there is the real likelihood that it will destroy the entire structure and all property. The lack of sanitary facilities makes the longhouse unhealthy. Some families say that they try to keep their family apartments cleaner and healthier than do others, for example, by spraying for bedbugs and roaches, while some families seem not to care.

A principal reason for the abandonment of the longhouse as a structural type and the construction of separate houses is the entrance of Iban into the "world" of the Chinese, Malays, and Europeans, whose settlement patterns they want to follow. Malay villages and rural Chinese communities comprise single family units, and the Iban who have built separate houses are among the most acculturated. A housing law in Sarawak, aimed at deterring Iban from abandoning the longhouse and putting up shantytowns, required that any separate residence had to cost at least $2,500. Thus, there is a certain prestige enjoyed by the family that has been able to afford to build a separate home.

It is important to note that in traditional Iban society those who lived apart were "evil spirited" *(Antu Uging)*. Thus the borrowing of models by more progressive Iban reveals a significant reversal of values.

Let me repeat, however that while there is an increase in the number of individual houses built by Iban in the downriver area and some even in upriver Sarawak, such as the Temenggong (Paramount Chief) Jugah's house at the mouth of the Ga'at River, there definitely is no mass abandonment of the longhouse system. To a majority of Iban, the longhouse still is the settlement pattern that is most meaningful culturally.

One final note of changes in Iban residence is to mention the new furnishings as tangible evidence of acculturation. Even in remote areas families have acquired Chinese-made cupboards, desks, tables, and imported, vinyl-covered furniture. I once slept in a spacious double bed at Nanga Entuloh, a full day's travel above Kapit. (Not all such acquisitions are improvements, however, as I learned one night when an Iban Pengulu insisted that I occupy his family's single bed—beneath which he had his mash for making rice beer—rather than sleep on the cool and airy verandah.) Signs of change take many forms, and following a two-hour, seven-mile walk over swamp bridged with saplings laid end to end, I found the walls of a family room of Rumah Ebom, Durin, covered with pictures from the *Asia Magazine*, *Time*, and an absolutely astounding array of centerfolds.

IBAN CULTURE

In their changing world, the Iban are seeing the devaluation of their traditional culture. Those capabilities and relations that were esteemed are being replaced with ones from abroad. The grammar of values has been altered so that among themselves Iban "do not speak the same language."

We have seen that the Iban was expected to be all things to all men, a man for all seasons, self-sufficient. Personal adequacy was demonstrated by the bringing in of trophies and by success in farming. This value has been preadaptive for those Iban who attempt to translate old idioms into new behavior. Instead of heads they now bring back money and other valuables such as sewing machines, outboard motors, and radios.

But some Iban who have been exposed to the specialization of Western technology and educated away from old values find themselves estranged from their people. One such young man who lived for several years in a boarding school admitted that he could never return to the longhouse because he was so un-schooled in local lore. He said: "When I tried to cut firewood, as other young men do every day, the girls laughed at me. I'll never go back to live in the longhouse because I cannot work as other men."

Fortunately, in his case the man was a superior student and is now well situated in the Borneo Development Office. Less fortunate are those Iban whose expectations have been raised by just enough education so that they will not—or cannot—farm, yet cannot find employment because of their low level of schooling. They congregate in the coffee shops, and have made a subculture of their own—one between the more successful and traditional culture of their parents and the more successful and modern culture of their peers.

The thoroughgoing egalitarian ethic of the Iban, holding in dynamic tension competition and cooperation, has provided a device for leveling members in each longhouse. It is recognized by more ambitious Iban as a major deterrent to their economic development, individually and corporately.

Not infrequently, Iban have preferred to see a Chinese prosper rather than one of their own group. In one situation I observed, a young man was given goods and a small amount of cash by the Development Office to open a shop in a remote area. He was industrious, his shop did well, and after three years he had several hundred dollars in a savings account. To the astonishment of a development officer who visited the area, the Iban demanded that the shop be closed. "But why?" asked the officer. "There is no other shop for half-a-day's travel, and he is serving you well, isn't he?" "Quite true," replied a spokesman for the other Iban, "but we don't want him 'eating us' (i.e., prospering at our expense)." Reluctantly, the development officer had to recommend that the shop be closed.

It is precisely such pressures that have led more than 3,000 Iban to open savings accounts in the banks of Sibu, and more acquisitive-minded Iban to conclude that they have no future in the longhouse. "What is the use of earning only to give it away?" asked one young man of Rumah Imba in a most reveal-ing question.

Those mechanisms, such as the *gawai* or festival system, which served to promote communal solidarity by requiring those who had to share with those who had not, are in jeopardy. When their application becomes intolerable to the young, the educated, the entrepreneurs, their effect is just the opposite of their intended purpose, as these and others move from the longhouse into Sibu or to Brunei, Sabah, or West Malaysia. The movements of such Iban marks a commitment to the value of achievement and a desire to be equal—but the equality now sought is with members of other cultures.

Although men have tended to be more mobile than women, especially during weeding activities, women also visit among themselves, or travel to towns to see the sights *(ngalu diri')* or to sell baskets and mats. It seems reasonable to explain much of such mobility as a means of escaping the tedium and tensions of "always being in sight and sound" of other community members, as well as to see old acquaintances and new places. The role of the prostitute, which does not conflict with the relaxed attitudes of Iban toward sex and which provides gainful employment not available otherwise to Iban women, has become that of several hundred such young women.

The adoption of values and styles of other ethnic groups is evidence of the cultural mobility of the Iban. Young men and women are sensitive to new styles seeking personal validation by the adoption of such fashions as long hair, hip-huggers, and —even in Sarawak's tropical climate—simulated leather jackets. Traditional dance patterns are still taught, but in some longhouses the rumba, twist, and "go-go dances" are studied by young adults in evening classes.

It is important to note that both old and new styles are continued according to the reactions of members of other ethnic groups, to whose values the Iban are adjusting. For example, Chinese and most Westerners have looked with some disdain on the practice of earlobe distention. In response to this negative opinion, scores of Iban, Kayan, and Kenyah have undergone minor surgery for the removal of the distended lobes. A second example is provided by a fad in the 1950s when Iban had their front teeth capped with gold, presumably for the cosmetic effect as well as to demonstrate wealth. This practice has disappeared, again because of negative reactions by members of other groups.

In the expanding world of the Iban there has occurred a shift in locus of cultural validation. Whereas traditionally such authority existed among the Iban themselves, their exposure to members of technologically superior groups has eroded confidence and fostered belief in the supremacy of the values of such groups.

The entrance of thousands of Iban into Christian churches provides, in some cases, examples of mobility and opportunism. During the past two decades more than 20,000 Iban in the Rejang Valley have been baptized and joined Christian churches, principally the Methodist and Roman Catholic denominations. Discussing the reasons for the entrance of a large group of Iban from Bawang Assan into the church, one of the community leaders stated:

Following the Japanese War, we were suspected of having collaborated with the Japanese. We knew that the British were Christians, and we wanted to be identified with them. So, after much discussion, we agreed that we could clear our names and show our identity with the British by becoming Christians.

Like the mutually supportive kin-groups, the church is looked upon as a benevolent fraternity. The church is looked to as an agency for help in time of need. More than a score of Iban whom I asked about their reasons for becoming Christians replied to the effect that

if we are not Christians, people won't take notice of us. If we are, we can get help. If we run out of money in town, we can borrow from someone. If we are sick, we can show our baptismal certificate and they will give us more powerful medicine at the hospital. We can get scholarships for our children. There are many advantages to being a Christian.

More sophisticated Iban who think less in terms of such immediate rewards feel that Christianity is a means to changing the total life situation through identification with members of a technologically superior society. A government officer said that he urged fellow Iban to become Christians so that they would become civilized and receive help from outside their own communities. He said:

If they don't become Christians, they will have to live by hunting and fishing. But if they become Christians, they can get employment for themselves and scholarships for their children.

The acceptance of Christianity by many Iban has been an additional means of gaining luck. The Christian faith is not accepted in place of but rather in addition to traditional beliefs and practices. The attitude of a majority of Christian Iban is that if being Christians brought good luck to the more technologically advanced Westerners, maybe it will do the same for us.

Thus it is understandable that the faith and practice of the Iban are syncretistic, with the Christian trinity placed alongside Iban gods. A common sight in many longhouses is a wooden cross on the door, over which hangs a dried leaf *(duan pinggan)* with mysterious markings in lime, or an offering basket *(kelingkang)*. On one occasion I observed a Christian service of "Sowing the Sacred Rice" *(Ngelaboh Padi Pun)* at 21 farms of families of Rumah Nyala. Following the service at his field, one man surreptitiously took a paper bag and returned to his field from that of another family. Thinking that he was unnoticed, he took a chicken that had been tied up from the bag, cut the chicken's throat, and poured the blood onto the ground, beseeching Pulang Gana to give him a good harvest. His rationale was that if one service would do some good, two would be even more helpful.

Contact with other ethnic groups and acculturation have begun to erode the faith of many Iban in their traditional rituals as of ensuring good luck. Augury is rapidly disappearing in the lower Rejang. The combined influences of Christianity and Western science have brought about a general loss of faith in the gods of the ancestors. In the words of one Iban farmer, "Our Pulang Gana now is in the Agriculture Department."

SUMMARY

The world of the Iban, whether in the hills or, more recently, on the plains, probably has never been completely integrated or wholly consistent. Numerous variations in belief and practice have existed. Nevertheless, as we have noted, the Iban shared common techniques, organizing principles, and values beneath their "canopy of culture heroes."

This traditional world now is being turned inside out, and new problems of consistency and integration are emerging. The setting of the Iban no longer can be defined in terms discussed in the first chapter. By travel, radio, and their own "interviews" conducted with foreign respondents, the Iban are citizens of "the world," sensitive to political developments in the Middle East and Ireland, intrigued with space travel, and concerned with market prices abroad.

The Iban are no longer politically dominant in their own state. Whereas they once moved at will and were the primary agents in their own creative activities, they now are caught by the forces of modernization. To move in work parties to another division requires administration approval. To live in their own land they must acknowledge the rule of others by the payment of taxes.

Even the form and functions of that elementary particle, the *bilik*-family, are changing. Marriage patterns, roles of support, the incidence of adoption, and forms of residence are responding to alien influences.

Nor is the longhouse universally the center of the world. Traditionalists confirm their commitment to this divinely decreed institution by building bigger and better longhouses, but constructed by Chinese or Malays. An increasing number, however, are—and more probably will be—erecting private dwellings, or even moving into Sarawak's towns.

The rivers of Sarawak are brown from soils exposed by farmers and loggers. But the erosion of confidence in many features of their culture threatens to sweep away much more that has been valuable and provided meaning. Alongside—in some instances in place of—Keling, Bungai Nuing, Pungga, Bungai Laja, and other gods stand Christ and Mohammed. No longer is rice cultivation the sole way of life; now money is a new resource to be obtained through adaptation to new niches, and as we have seen the entire concept of work has been redefined in terms of wage earning.

The "life-plan" that once clearly prescribed the way to success and self-esteem through pioneering, head-hunting, and farming is now in conflict with and obscured by other "life-plans" prescribing education, employment, trade, and foreign travel, realizable in some cases, but not in others. Hence, some Iban find adjustment to new demands and expectations stressful. Alcoholic drinks, such as beer, whiskey, and brandy, previously consumed exclusively on festival occasions when the social order was suspended, are the daily fare—in some cases in staggering quantities—of some Iban for whom coping is difficult.

Evidence of such stress is exceptional, however. For most Iban, adjustments are being made with few apparent difficulties. The worlds they have known in the hills and on the plains are now being transformed by the new universe into which they have been drawn, and the Iban are finding new areas in which to expand and new meanings for their lives as "The People."

Epilogue

THE 1970s AND THE 1980s

In 1984, the author, supported by a Fulbright grant, returned to conduct research on Iban urban migration into Sibu. As long as he had lived in Sibu between 1957 and 1972, and as thoroughly acquainted as he was with its population, nothing could have prepared him for the dramatic changes which have occurred during the past two decades.

The Sibu Urban Area has grown from 20 square miles in 1970 to a Municipal Area (as described by the Mayor) of 50 square miles in 1984. The population of the Sibu Urban District Council was 86,680 in 1980 and, combined with the Sibu Rural District population, 134,786.

Of interest to us are Iban migrants. In the 1980 Census, 6,797 Iban were enumerated in the Sibu Urban District population. Extrapolating to 1984, we estimate the Iban population in Sibu to be 8,100. These are figures provided by the Department of Statistics, and ones the author finds problematic. They are reminiscent of the observation of a Filipino sociologist, that ''there are few things easier to collect in Southeast Asia than incorrect statistics.''

For example, Iban youth in particular are highly mobile and

apt to be missed in enumerations. Sixty-eight percent of Iban I contacted were 18 years of age or younger (1,374). Eighty-five percent of that number (1,160) are still in school, and the others (214) describe their situations as jobless, as living with relatives or friends, or simply in town to look things over. This cohort of the Iban population requires careful attention because (1) it is likely to yield permanent residents for the town and (2) its constituents are learning a new value system, one in which they are being provided for by government scholarship (as is the case of students) or by relatives or friends, without any assumption of responsibility for their lives.

The changes of the 1970s and 1980s may be summarized in four categories: settlement patterns, occupations, roles, and relations. By implication, these changes have affected and will affect the identity and values of Iban. We shall consider each change in turn.

Urban migration has abrogated the once normative patterns of longhouse residence, and familiar measures of "the true Iban" no longer hold. Contrary to stereotypes held by Chinese or Malays of Iban as "upriver, longhouse dwellers," these are no longer true. The identity of Iban in Sibu is not based upon a particular residence pattern, but on the practice of a common culture and use of the same primary language.

Movement into Sibu has been marked by the predominance of separate dwellings and settlement among members of other ethnic groups. As described earlier, Iban live in quarters provided by employers, own their own lot and house, or, in common with other Third World towns, they live in squatters settlements. Renting is a fourth alternative, but in Sibu a relatively expensive proposition with no permanent return.

Except for Iban who are provided housing or those who can afford to purchase a tract of land and build their own home, squatting is preferred by about 1,500 migrants. In 1984 there were four squatters settlements. One was a "legal" settlement, built by workers on land owned by their employer. The oldest settlement is at Pulau Babi, having been established almost two decades ago as a "temporary" location. At the time of this research the families were still there.

The squatters settlement at Usaha Jaya east of Sibu is the largest, most complex, and best organized. It is representative of squatments throughout the Third World in which migrants take upon themselves the solutions to their housing problems,

Iban Squatters at Upper Lanang Squatter Area

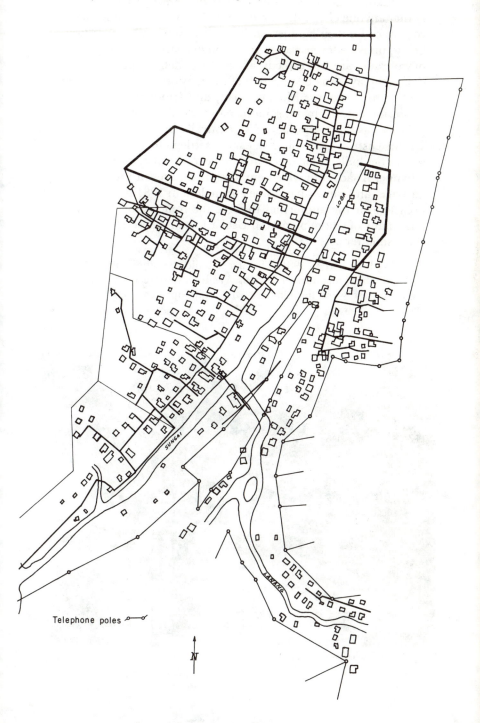

Telephone poles ⚬—⚬

N

recognizing that unless they take care of themselves it is unlikely that anyone else will. These are people who are immediately concerned for their families' shelter, protection, and general well-being, unlike administrators who though charged with oversight of migrants are not directly affected by their plights.

Usaha Jaya was begun in 1980, a community formed from three ethnic groups: Malays, Iban, and Chinese. Prior to its establishment, the major squatment was a collection of "floating palaces" as they were named sarcastically by a member of the Urban District Council. The earlier settlement was comprised of shanties built on logs anchored in the town's major drain along Channel Road, into which emptied discharges of raw sewage, garbage, and rain. An outbreak of cholera in 1981 provided the occasion for the authorities to force the removal of the squatters, many of whom pioneered Usaha Jaya. As described by two Iban squatters:

> We built here in 1981. The first to build were the Malays, who built just upriver from us. We Iban were second, and the last were the Chinese who built upriver from the

Walkway into Usaha Jaya at high tide.

Malays. When the first families wanted to build here, the Government told them not to. They went ahead anyway, and "enforcers" from Land and Survey sawed the supporting timbers. Seeing that, they rebuilt and the enforcers cut the timbers again. Once, however, 20 families built overnight and, confronted with the determination and sheer numbers, the Land and Survey people let us stay.

Seeing a lot of us having built here, we believe the administrators had a meeting. From that, they surveyed the land and made out a site-plan. Each lot is 10 fathoms square. They also fixed the size of each house. After they had surveyed the lots, they urged people to get their lot numbers, because they were going to limit relocation here. Therefore, a lot of people, including the Chinese upriver, asked for lots. Officially, building was to have stopped in 1983, but there are still people constructing houses, as you can see. And because they don't have lot numbers, some people have crowded their houses in between others.

Squatters build on empty land because they are fleeing rural poverty and inadequate services in most cases. They are convinced that there are greater opportunities available to them in towns and cities. Theirs is an insecure existence. They do not have title to land and little prospect of obtaining it. "We do not know what is going to become of us, whether we should improve our homes, invest more in developing our lives here, or save in anticipation of being relocated," one lamented.

Despite the multiethnic, pluralistic communities in which they are living, it is important to note the persistence of some features of Iban culture, other than language and basic values. These include:

- retention of customary rights to land and concern about obtaining title to land held under usufruct;
- labor exchange in house-building and in the occasional agricultural activities of women and men;
- the dedication of significant activities through traditional rituals, for example, the sacrifice of a chicken on a center post of a squatter's house;
- weekend "happy hours" in one another's houses, and the inclusion of wives in the festivities;
- exchange visits whenever possible for participation in longhouse rituals;

- hospitality to guests, and especially members of one's own kindred or "brotherhood";
- mutual gift-giving, most commonly remittances of cash from employed squatters to parents or siblings in rural areas, and gifts of produce or even machinery, e.g., a generator, to squatters from relatively well-off rural kin.

The second category of changes occurring among Iban in the past twenty years is the growing importance of cash. What people grow up without may be as important as, or more important than, what they grow up with. I am currently writing the biography of the last Paramount Chief of the Iban, Tun Temenggong Jugah, a man well-known for his frugality which may be attributed to the fact that cash was almost impossible for the late Tun to acquire in his early years.

The discussion of cash as a new factor in the value system of the Iban may be extended with two incidents which occurred in 1984. First, while doing research at the request of the Sarawak Museum on Iban-Kajang relations in an upriver area, I observed an Iban loading a deer onto a launch for sale in a port town. "I would like to share this deer with the people of my community," he expalined apologetically, "but I need the money. Besides, why should I share with them? If they had been lucky enough to shoot it, they wouldn't share with me!" This was in stark contrast to experiences I had in the 1960s when an eleven-foot python was killed below Rumah Gaong, another occasion when deer were shot, and still another when pigs were killed as they swam in a nearby river. All shared equally in that game. But not necessarily so any more.

The second incident occurred over the weekend of July 4 and 5, 1984, when Iban of Bawang Assan observed the Festival of the Spirits (*Gawai Antu*). Although this festival is less important in other divisions than it is in the First and Second Divisions, it still has been a major festival even in the Rejang Valley. The major purpose of the Gawai is to give secondary burials to all deceased Iban who have not been so honored. More than that, the festival encapsulates Iban cosmology and eschatology, uniting time and eternity, the living and the dead, earth and non-earth (*Sebayan*). Having attended a festival in the Second Division in 1970, I looked forward to the pageantry and rich ritual in Bawang Assan. But it was an economic affair, with little ritual and no pageantry. Communal meals, drinking, cockfighting and "housing" the dead constituted the entire festival. When I inquired about the truncated ceremony, one of the organizers said that they had not hired bards "because they are too expensive" and more pageantry was not included "because we can't afford the time."

According to the 1980 Population Census, 7.7 percent of the 10,130 Iban enumerated in urban areas were there because of a job offer. Another source (Hamid Bugo, 1984) states that 66 percent of Iban urban migrants moved into Sarawak's towns looking for employment. Despite the obvious disagreement of these figures, there is no question that thousands of Iban have moved into urban areas seeking cash-paying jobs.

In Sibu, Iban fill a broad range of occupations. At the time of this research, the Resident of the Third Division was an Iban. There were Iban professionals, educated and working as lawyers, doctors, clergy and teachers, businessmen, and in almost every government department. A majority of Police, Field Force, and Border Scouts in my survey were Iban. Iban also comprised a large portion of the unskilled labor force, working as laborers in the numerous construction projects.

A cruel irony in light of the primary attraction of cash is that rising expectations also incur rising expenses. Many urban migrants have found that everything in town costs money, and that there is not enough money to buy everything they want or even need.

The desire for an urban life-style has led to "the two paycheck family." Wives must work if the family is to fulfill its dream of the good life, equipped with radio, television, and other material things. Every family in my survey had a radio, and a majority either owned or had access to a television set. Iban have quickly grasped the availability of credit, and some are quite willing to mortgage the future as they buy now and pay later.

Upon arrival in Sibu in 1984, I was advised that I should give some attention to the number of Iban prostitutes. Within the first week, I had begun a series of interviews, first with two prostitutes to whom I was introduced by some acquaintances, then, with almost two dozen others who were brought into the police headquarters for interrogation. Contrary to some notions about prostitution, all those interviewed except two indicated that they practiced it as a matter of choice. (Candidly, there appeared few other choices as rewarding monetarily.) There are an estimated

Early morning traffic in Sibu, with Volvos and Mercedes in abundance.

400 to 800 Iban prostitutes who come and go in Sibu. Their ages ranged from 12 to 35 years of age, and they came from all of Sarawak's seven divisions. Many came from economically depressed areas and claimed there was no work or economic opportunities for them in their longhouses.

Restriction of prostitution and rehabilitation of the women involved appear difficult if not impossible. At the time of the research, the police conducted twice-weekly raids between 7:30 and 9:00 p.m. on Mondays and Wednesdays. These times were determined by the availability of a health inspector who examined the women for "sexually transmitted diseases." (Somewhat surprisingly, only four prostitutes were diagnosed as having a sexually transmitted disease in 1983 data.)

Inasmuch as prostitution is a matter of choice (given limited or non-existent alternatives) permitting women to work as they want, when they want, and where they want, and is financially rewarding, it undoubtedly will continue. In order to determine whether there is psychological damage suffered by Iban prostitutes, studies of self-image, esteem, and sense of self-worth would have to be done. Though much of their efforts may be part of a Goffman-type face game, the Iban prostitutes I observed daily were generally happy, pleasant, and confident. In their interviews, a majority indicated that they had been abused or abandoned, and that prostitution was a way by which they could get what they wanted with no obligation to anyone else.

The third category of change among Sibu Iban is that of role differentiation. Typical of all urban societies, Sibu's has evolved institutions necessary for the acquisition, distribution, and provision of goods and services to its population. The evolution of these institutions has been accompanied by new roles. Of significance to our concern here is that Iban are to be found in virtually every one. In my 1984 survey I found Iban in every government agency, and in increasing numbers in the private sector.

Role differentiation is an obvious contrast to the limited positions and roles of Iban in rural areas, where both men and women farmed, where men collected commercially valuable products and women wove blankets and baskets. Men occasionally left longhouses for work as seasonal laborers, or signed on for multi-year jobs in other parts of the state. But in comparison with the numerous agencies and institutions of Sibu, relatively few positions were available to rural Iban.

Differentiation of roles and rewards is related to differentiation in relations as well. Historically Iban have lived and worked with fellow Iban. They have exchanged labor during the critical farming periods, ideas during the long evening conversations, and visits during the numerous ritual events which served to maintain ties over time and space. Only occasionally did Iban have contact or interact with non-Iban. All of this has changed among urbanizing Iban. In the shipyard, the bank, the office, or school, Iban are living and working with non-Iban. Exchanges are now between members of different ethnic groups, and contacts and interactions with fellow Iban are restricted to home or social occasions.

As they experience differentiation of roles, rewards, and relations, how will Iban maintain their sense of ethnic identity? The intensity of their identification process has lain in the frequency of cues in a cultural code which continuously reaffirmed their Ibanness. Though they may continue to speak the language and refer to traditional values, will the ethnic identity of the Iban become secondary to other criteria and conditions of identification? Will the Iban, as American citizens, assume a new primary identity of Malaysia while maintaining the pride of a cultural heritage which contributes to a richer fabric of national citizen?

Finally, what are the aspirations of urbanizing Iban? It is both perilous and presumptuous on my part, as occasional observer, to speak to the dreams and expectations of a people as diverse as the Iban. There are Iban and there are Iban, just as there are Americans and Americans. Differences in aspirations among Iban are no less than those between Americans. But this is my assignment, and with the cautions noted above, let me attempt to enumerate Iban aspirations.

First, most Iban want adequate rewards from their lives and work. Participating in a monetized economy, they certainly want a fair wage, enough to buy food, to provide clothing and shelter, and to live beyond the stress of enervating anxiety about money. But they also want a sense of purpose from their work, a belief that they are participating in and contributing to the development of their families, their society, and state. One of the tasks of every society is to convince its members that life is worth living, and worth living in particular ways. This social task can only be accomplished when human beings know themselves to be sharing in ways of life or programs which are greater than themselves.

Hotel and Caterpillar dealership in upriver town of Kapit, owned and operated by Iban.

In her analysis of *The Human Condition*, the late Hannah Arendt distinguished between work, labor, and vocation. Work is effort expended by a person who is effectively in control of his situation. Iban farmers performed "work" according to their own schedules, decided their own tasks, were more or less "masters of their own fates." Labor, according to Arendt, is the exchange of human time and energy for monetary reward. Labor in particular may be stressful and frustrating for lack of opportunity to learn, to develop, to grow. Vocation is purposeful activity which transcends both work and labor. With intentions which go beyond the mere performance of a task or the simple exchange of time and energy, the person is rewarded by a sense of self- and task-transcendence, as much as by wages or other material benefits. In a vocation, persons discover what they enjoy doing and, happily, are compensated for doing their tasks.

Second, Iban want adequate shelter and land. Of all issues among urbanizing Iban, probably none is of greater importance and sensitivity than that of land ownership, land-rights, and security of residence. In 1987 the United Nations observed The Year of Shelter. An increasing percentage of the world's people suffer for lack of adequate shelter. In the United States, street people, people who live on our cities' streets, some, their entire lives, are a challenge to and indictment of our social programs. Currently, we are planning publication of an issue of our journal, *Studies in Third World Societies,* on street children of the Third World. There are millions of them. Mercifully, Sarawak enjoys a moderate climate and social support system so urban migrants do not freeze to death or have to live on the streets. But squatters want title to land, and some commitment from local and state government agencies that will give them security in establishing their residences.

Third, Iban want adequate participation in decision-making activities, particularly political processes, which affect them. In longhouse communities, decisions were made by consultation, discussion, and, ideally, consensus. All who might be affected by a decision were involved in consideration of issues and their implications. (This strategy of "participatory management" is remarkably modern; many management experts advise consulting managers and staff prior to making decisions. Otherwise, persons become aggrieved and disaffected when decisions are made *for* them rather than *with* them.)

A challenge facing government is determining "who speaks

for the Iban.'' A characteristic of state government is the pluralism of positions, frequently competing and conflicting voices representing to speak for the same constituency. The state government is to be commended for permitting dialogue and debate in its efforts to achieve greater participation in decision-making. Such participation is necessary in a people-oriented political process. Winston Churchill once commented that ''democracy is the worst of political systems, unless one considers the alternatives.''

Fourth, urbanizing Iban want confirmation of their history and of themselves as people of worth and dignity. The Iban have been a dynamic and remarkably creative people, who, during the past two centuries, have expanded into all parts of northern Borneo. Whether they will be able to retain their sense of unity and ethnic identity, whether they will be able to maintain their values, whether they will support the rich traditions which have made them one of the most interesting societies in Southeast Asia, are questions which must await time, and assessment through new research in the future.

Additional Bibliographic Citation:

Bugo, Hamid. *The Economic Development of Sarawak,* Kuching, Sarawak, 1984.

BIBLIOGRAPHY

Government Publications and Papers

Annual Report of the Department of Agriculture, Third Division, Upper Rejang, for the Year 1970. Sibu: mimeographed.

Banks, E. *Bornean Mammals.* Kuching: The Kuching Press, 1949.

Browne, F. G. *Forest Trees of Sarawak and Brunei and Their Products.* Kuching: Government Printer, 1955.

Jones, L. W. *Sarawak, Report on the Census of Population Taken on June 15, 1960.* Kuching: Government Printing Office, 1963.

Noakes, J. L. *Sarawak, Report on the Census of Population Taken on June 15, 1960.* Kuching: Government Printing Office, 1963.

Scott, I. M. *Report on a Detailed Soil Survey of Oya Road Agricultural Station, Third Division.* Kuching: Department of Agriculture (mimeographed), 1964.

———— *Report on a Semi-Detailed Soil Survey of the Forest Experimental Nursery Oya Road, Third Division.* Kuching: Department of Agriculture (mimeographed), 1965.

———— *Report on Semi-Detailed Soil Surveys of Proposed Sites for a Peat Research Station in Sibu District, Third Division.* Kuching: Department of Agriculture (mimeographed), December 1969.

Books and Periodicals

Allen, Betty M. *Malayan Fruits.* Singapore: Donald Moore Press, 1970.

Anderson, J. A. R. "The Structure and Development of the Peat Swamps of Sarawak and Brunei," *Journal of Tropical Geography*, 18: 7–16, 1964.

Beavitt, Paul. "Ngayap," *Sarawak Museum Journal*, XV (New Series Nos. 30–31): 407–413, 1967.

Brooke, Charles. *Ten Years in Sarawak.* London: Tinsley Brothers, 1866.

Chagnon, Napoleon. *Studying the Yanomamo.* New York: Holt, Rinehart and Winston, Inc., 1974.

Douglas, Mary. "Pollution," *International Encyclopedia of the Social Sciences*, David L. Sills, Ed. New York: Crowell Collier Macmillan, Inc., Vol. XII: 336–341, 1968.

Freeman, J. D. *Iban Agriculture.* London: Her Majesty's Stationery Office, 1955.

———— "The Iban of West Borneo," in G. P. Murdock, Ed., *Social Structure in Southeast Asia.* Chicago: Quadrangle Books, 1960.

———— "On the Concept of the Kindred," *Journal of the Royal Anthropological Institute*, 91: 192–207, 1961.

———— *Report on the Iban.* London: The Athlone Press, 1970.

Gerijih, Henry. *Raja Langit.* Kuching: Borneo Literature Bureau, 1964.

Goffman, Erving. *Interaction Ritual.* Garden City, N.Y.: Doubleday and Company, Inc., 1967.

Harrisson, T. H. "The 'Palang,' Its History and Proto-History in West Borneo and the Philippines," *Journal of the Malaysian Branch of the Royal Anthropological Society*, Vol. XXXVII, Pt. 2: 162–173, 1964.

———— *The Malays of South-West Sarawak Before Malaysia.* London: Macmillan, 1970.

Jackson, James. *Sarawak: A Geographical Survey of a Developing State.* London: University of London Press, 1968.

Lande, C. H. *Leaders, Factions, and Parties: The Structure of Philippine Politics.* Southeast Asia Studies, Yale University, Monograph Series No. 6, 1964.

McKinley, Robert. "Human and Proud of It." Paper presented to Symposium of the Borneo Research Council, American Anthropological Association, New Orleans, November 30, 1973.

Parsons, David. "A History of Forest Industries in Sarawak," *The Sarawak Teacher*, pp. 6–10, 1966, Sibu: Education Office.

Pelzer, Karl J. *Pioneer Settlement in the Asiatic Tropics.* New York: American Geographical Society, 1945.

Pringle, Robert. *Rajahs and Rebels.* London: Macmillan, 1970.

Roth, Henry Ling. *The Natives of Sarawak and British North Borneo*, Kuala Lumpur: University of Malaya Press, 1968.

Sahlins, Marshall. "Poor Man, Rich Man, Big-Man, Chief: Political Types in Melanesia and Polynesia," *Comparative Studies in Society and History*, Vol. 5, No. 3, April 1963.

Salisbury, R. F. "Unilineal Descent in the New Guinea Highlands," *Man*, Vol. 56, 1956.

Sandin, Benedict. *Sengalang Burong.* Kuching: Borneo Literature Bureau, 1962, 1967.

Schwenk, Richard. "Agricultural Development in the Upper Rejang Valley," *Studies in Third World Societies*, Publication No. 3 (in press).

"Sarawak Family Planning Association, 1970 (Sibu Branch)." Sibu: mimeographed, 1970.

Smythies, B. E. *The Birds of Borneo.* London: Oliver and Boyd, 1960.

Spiro, Melford. "Ghosts, Ifaluk, and Teleological Functionalism," *American Anthropologist*, 54: 497–503, 1952.

Srinivas, M. N. and A. Beteille. "Networks in Indian Social Structure," *Man*, 64: 165–168, 1964.

Newspapers

The Borneo Bulletin

Sarawak Gazette, 1870–1970

Sarawak Tribune

See Hua Daily News

Straits Times (Malaysian Edition)

The Vanguard

GLOSSARY

antu   non-human spirits

bilik-family   usually, parents and children, often including grandparents, who reside in the *bilik* of a longhouse, sharing rights to land and other resources

derris root   a leguminous plant, *Derris elliptica,* containing rotenone and used to stun fish

dibble-stick   a fire-hardened pointed stick poked into the soil of hill farms to make holes into which rice seed are placed

dipterocarps   a family of trees peculiar to Southeast Asia

dry rice   rice grown usually in upland areas in unirrigated fields

dunya   earth, the world

gawai   festival

Imperata cylindrica   one of several grasses which invade hill farms and, in a few years, change rice fields into "green deserts"

kaban belayan   the company of kinspeople, an amorphous group less defined than the *suku juru*

leaching   the downward illuviation of nutrients, especially in cleared areas in which the soil is exposed to the full impact of tropical rains

longhouse   an attenuated structure with as few as seven and as many as 80 family units; each longhouse is usually centered around a core of cognatic kin

menoa tasik   land(s) beyond the sea

mensia mayoh   the masses, commoners

mensia saribu   the thousands, also refers to commoners

musin kamarau   the short dry season between the southwest and northeast monsoons musin landas   the rainy seasons of the monsoons

nonsororal polygyny   the marriage of one man to two women who are not sisters

padi   rice

padong   a raised platform on the outer section of the covered verandah of a longhouse

para rubber   *Hevea brasiliensis,* or rubber produced by trees of the genus Siphonia, native to Brazil and introduced into Southeast Asia in the late nineteenth century

petara   gods or semi-divine beings

Pulang Gana   the god of land, fertility and horticulture

raja berani   the brave (and) rich

ruai   the covered verandah of a longhouse

rumah   house

samengat   soul, bounded spirit

sebayan   "the Opposite," the afterworld

shaman   an ecstatic, psythotherapist, specialist of the soul

sororal polygyny   marriage of one man to two women who are sisters

suku juru   the ego-centered kindred, those persons who might be expected to share in the major events in a person's life

tanju'   uncovered porch in front of longhouse

ulun berani   a captured slave

ulun leka rian   a slave through indebtedness

wet rice   rice grown in irrigated fields

Index